Coping
with
Calamities

Coping with Calamities

Survival strategies for leaders

Sarah W. Fraser

Kingsham

First published in 2004
by Kingsham Press

Oldbury Complex
Marsh Lane
Easthampnett
Chichester, West Sussex
PO18 OJW
United Kingdom

Typeset in AGaramond

Printed and bound by
Antony Rowe Ltd
Chippenham
Wiltshire
United Kingdom

ISBN: 1-904235-25-5

British Library Cataloging in Publication Data
A catalogue record of this book is available from the British Library

Fraser, Sarah.

This book is dedicated
to
The Rotary Club of Aylesbury
Buckinghamshire
England

When I committed to writing this book, I imagined listening to a few stories and then writing them up, analysing them and doing some editing. I perceived it as an exercise in writing, which to some extent it was. However, I was completely unprepared for the emotional depth and richness of the personal experiences shared by my fellow Rotarians.

Every one of these stories has taken great courage to share, with the humility to reflect and express the personal lessons learnt. This has been done with two purposes in mind; to help others learn the lessons of coping with everyday calamities, and to support the production of a book where the profits will be diverted to charitable giving through the International Rotary Foundation.

There are many ways to fulfil charitable obligations. Raising money and passing this on to specialist organisations that manage it where it is needed is one such way, such as the Rotary Foundation using money raised from this book to help eradicate polio in the world. Another form of giving is, to give of your time and your self. Every contribution in this book represents this aspect.

I would like to dedicate this book to all those who give freely of their time and their expertise. To the school children who raise funds to travel to distant lands to paint hospital walls, to youngsters who choose to spend their gap year helping build houses in places far from their own homes, and to those who take the time to sit with our elders in local community homes or to fix the plumbing in the local charity shop.

In giving of themselves they truly appreciate the nature of gift; that in giving they also receive.

Sarah Fraser
2004

Contents

Foreword xi
Overview xv

Chapter 1 "Small things matter" **1**
    Introduction 1
    Key themes 1
    Leadership reflections 4
    Conclusion 7
    Annotated bibliography and references 7

Chapter 2 "Rallying round" **9**
    Introduction 9
    Key themes 9
    Personal experience 10
    Leadership reflections 11
    Commentary 15
    Conclusion 15
    Annotated bibliography and references 16

Chapter 3 "Big events, big decisions" **17**
    Introduction 17
    Key themes 17
    Personal experience 19
    Conclusion 23
    Post script 24
    Annotated bibliography and references 24

Chapter 4 "Legal liabilities" **25**
    Introduction 25
    Key themes 25
    Personal experience 25
    Conclusion 29
    Annotated bibliography and references 29

Chapter 5 "Family matters" **31**
    Introduction 31
    Key themes 31
    Personal experience 32
    Conclusion 35
    Annotated bibliography and references 35

Chapter 6   **"Charities; cash counts"** 37
Introduction 37
Key themes 37
Personal experience 38
Conclusion 41
Annotated bibliography and references 41

Chapter 7   **"Overblown"** 43
Introduction 43
Key themes 43
Personal experience 44
Conclusion 48
Annotated bibliography and references 48

Chapter 8   **A "locky" business"** 49
Introduction 49
Key themes 49
Personal experience 50
Conclusion 53
Annotated bibliography and references 53

Chapter 9   **"Gaining from losing"** 55
Introduction 55
Key themes 55
Personal experience 56
Commentary by Sarah Fraser 59
Conclusion 60
Annotated bibliography and references 60

Chapter 10 **"Risky business"** 61
Introduction 61
Key themes 61
Personal experience 62
Conclusion 65
Annotated bibliography and references 65

Chapter 11 **"Spilt milk"** 67
Introduction 67
Key themes 67
Personal experience 68
Conclusion 70
Annotated bibliography and references 71

Chapter 12 **"In the public eye"** 73
Introduction 73
Key themes 73
Personal experience 74
Conclusion 77
Annotated bibliography and references 77

Chapter 13 "The importance of pause" . . . . **.79**
    Introduction 79
    Key themes 79
    Personal experience 80
    Conclusion 85
    Annotated bibliography and references 85

Chapter 14 "Rain or shine" . . . . **.87**
    Introduction 87
    Key themes 87
    Personal experience 88
    Conclusion 89
    Annotated bibliography and references 90

About Rotary 91

Foreword

As a youngster when I was into complaining about one thing or another, and about how unfair life was, my mother used to feed me that familiar line: *If life gives you a bunch of lemons, make lemonade.* Life has given me my share of lemons and, gratefully, the wisdom to realise that, what at the time left the most sour of tastes in my mouth, was later to prove to be the sweetest of blessings in disguise.

So when Sarah Fraser asked me if I would write a forward to the book on "Coping with Calamities", I felt honoured. It wasn't until I'd read the first few chapters others had contributed that I realised what a challenge I'd set for myself. Here was a group of men and women who were willing to open their hearts and expose some very deeply personal and moving experiences of how, having been dealt a full measure of lemons, they created over-flowing jugs of lemonade. To share one's experience and strength in turning pain into gain, and calamity into wisdom, was reflective of hearts and souls that knew a humility and grace that most assuredly was at the core of all that is good and right about servant leadership. The kind of servant leadership that has spawned and sustained the many Rotary Clubs around the world.

As you read the stories in this book, don't be surprised if you occasionally feel a knot develop in your stomach. A bit of sweat coating your palms. A knowing grin cross your lips. For the real power of these stories is the reminder that calamities bring us the gift of a renewed and ever deepening sense of faith and hope. Faith that the bigger and darker the shadow, like that cast by a lunar eclipse of the sun, the more powerful is the light which is momentarily being blocked. Hope that, by treating each moment as a learning experience, and each breath as the gift that it is, we will continue to accept life on life's terms. For by so doing, as an ancient prayer compels us, we strengthen the possibility that we may be granted the serenity to accept the things we cannot change, the courage to change the things we can, and the wisdom to know the difference.

The many courageous contributors to this volume have given us just such an extraordinary gift indeed. We can honour their courage by telling our own stories of challenge, of over-coming adversity, of lemons turned into lemonade. In so doing, others close to us can feel the same sense of renewed faith and hope. It is in the spirit of such a willingness to lead by example that I humbly offer my own story of how a series of seeming calamities have served to forge and mark the path that has proven to be my personal calling.

The little engine that could

One of the things that I have always valued about myself and that other people have valued about me is my ability to sense what's going on in a group relatively quickly.

The seeds were planted early in childhood. As a youngster, growing up in my household meant spending many evenings, baited breath, while sitting at the dining room table vigilantly sensing the raging bull. With a violent, domineering father, explosions were a regular occurrence and landmines to be avoided. It took the most well developed and highly sensitive radar to detect an imminent shift in personality and feel the kinetic threat. With laser precision, I could sense the energy shifts within the family, within the group; if I didn't sense things correctly, and know exactly when and how to intervene, blood would be shed. From these early developmental roots I became quite adept at sensing, spotting, and understanding covert dynamics within groups and ultimately the value of a well-developed competency for addressing healthy conflict toward learning and growth.

Finding myself a graduate student at MIT, more from conflict avoidance – not wanting to confront my father with my lacklustre desire for a future with the family business – than anything else, I found myself in an organisation behaviour class in management school. I'll never forget that first day in that required class. Don Marquis, a senior faculty person, a left-brain non-touchy-feely wonderful person, was teaching the class.

Here we were, a group of engineering students and scientists, and Dr. Marquis had the nerve to tell us that he was going to run an experiential simulation with the class and then stated: "Here are what the results of the simulation are going to be." I can still close my eyes and see myself in that classroom thinking to myself – "What a dumbo! How could he possibly expect to be able to get away with telling us the results and *then* running the damn experiment?!"

It was an experiment in inter-group competition, it was the classic Ash Group Dynamics experiment. The results predicted that moments after two groups were formed [on a purely random basis, at that!] the members of each group would begin to see themselves as superior on a host of subjective dimensions [e.g., fairness, competence, etc.,] compared to the members of the other group. And, of course, knowing the data did nothing but exacerbate the results! After that experiential simulation, at the end of that class, I knew there was far more to this stuff than I ever imagined. Don Marquis had really jolted me into an appreciation for the science of human behaviour.

The slow climb continued…

Shortly after that experience and insight I realized there's no way the traditional classroom teaches integrity. The kind of integrity that one's personal being can carry in the world. The integrity involved in *being* a human *being*. *You* don't learn this in the classroom or through some course – you learn this through following somebody's example in life. This is what Douglas McGregor contributed to my unfolding journey of awareness.

Douglas McGregor was a pioneer in the field of human behaviour in organisations and a professor at MIT during my doctoral pursuits. As a part of the Ph.D. requirements at Massachusetts Institute of Technology, all candidates had to pass an oral examination. This traditional rite of passage, conducted by the department's senior faculty, had the well-earned reputation of being the equivalent of "intellectual hell week."

Two hours before my own trial by fire, Doug came to me and announced that he intended to initiate a "minor" change in the process. The faculty grilling of the novitiate felt too incongruous to Doug, a man whose life was built around a set of values based on treating all human beings like the gifts of our Creator that they were. So instead of being treated like a second-class citizen, I was to "act like a professor" and give a group of students (the likes, mind you, of Warren Bennis, Edgar Schein, Donald Marquis, and other forefathers of the management and organisational behaviour field) a brief lecture on my theory of human behaviour in organisations.

While I do not recall any of the details of how I spent the next two hours (except that most of the time I was in the men's room!), I do remember very vividly the opening sixty seconds of my first formal lecture. After Doug announced the change in process (to the chagrin, I must say, of some staunch traditionalists), he simply turned to me with a smile and nodded non-verbally, "Go for it!"

I took a deep breath and thanked him, trying to sound as sincere as I could. In a painful statement of the obvious, I then admitted to a high degree of nervousness and anxiety. After managing to swallow back my raw fear for a second, I spat out the words: "So much of what I have to say, Doug, has been influenced by your thinking and writing that I'm afraid this lecture is going to sound very redundant. I apologise."

Doug then shifted his ever-present pipe to his left hand and rested his chin in the space between his right thumb and second finger, a trademark signal that he was about to deliver some thoughtful feedback, with the consummate skill and delicacy he wrote about being essential to any and every "performance appraisal" situation.

To this day I can close my eyes and see the warm smile on his face and hear the love and compassion in his voice as he responded, "I hope you won't let my presence influence you, Irv, for I fully expect to learn something new today." Doug McGregor, with the integrity he lived and breathed, gave me voice. Doug allowed me to bring to bear my own experience to the concepts that he provided; that somebody listening to the intellectual content as it resonated through my heart might, in fact, begin to be able to take something for themselves into their heart.

Congruency. Doug McGregor, a man who walked his talk, taught me the deep importance of having physical, emotional, intellectual, and spiritual integrity in this world. Now I had the pieces – the fun learning ready for harvest. Today, that keen radar deep inside, just above my belly button, is one of my most highly prized instruments for aiding executives or individuals along their paths, not to mention the greatest challenges of helping myself!

By being who we are and maturing into who we want to be, our fears can be confronted and developed with delicacy and skill and released for positive growth. The ability to fully sense when someone is ready for that release and facilitate his or her alignment with humility has brought integrity to my being.

And the slow climb continues… one day at a time.

Dr Irv Rubin

Overview

This book is about three important words: *coping*, *calamity* and *leader*. Each of these has a dictionary definition and each is also very specific to the context within which they are used and subject to the perceptions of those who use them.

"*Coping*" is defined by the Oxford English Dictionary as to *contend evenly, grapple successfully*. It is about recovery, about making it through the difficult times or over the obstacles. Implicit within coping, is the notion of *survival*, of being able to continue.

"**Calamity**" is defined as *adversity* or *deep distress*. This is a highly subjective notion and the amount of distress differs per person as to whether they would then classify an adverse event as a calamity. It's a personal matter.

So who is a "**Leader**"? This book is based on the premise that we are all leaders. Some of us hold formal positional roles that we use to define ourselves as leaders, for others it is more subtle. Everyone in this book has demonstrated leadership within his or her community. Every person in this book is an ordinary leader – for whom ordinary, and sometimes extra-ordinary, mishaps happen. There are many books that cover the high profile leaders in the world. Our aim is to share with you what happens when every day leaders meet every day calamities, and how they cope with them.

And who are these every day leaders? Each chapter in this book is an account of a calamity as experienced by a member of the Rotary Club of Aylesbury in England. This book demonstrates the breadth of membership in Rotary throughout the world and depth of the experience of members, as well as their commitment to share their stories so others may learn.

In "**Small things matter**", Dr Roger Bodley tells his story of leaving a needle exposed and the ensuing injury sustained by a cleaner. He learnt how small things can have a huge impact and how inspection and protocols can reduce error rates, but not avoid them entirely. He also experienced the dilemma of whether to own up to the fact that he was the person who left the needle on the counter.

Des May shares his experience in the second chapter, "**Rallying round**" when, as Head Teacher, part of his school was burnt down in an arson attack. His story shows how calamities can bring out the best in communities and the importance of keeping "the show on the road".

In **"Big events, big decisions"** James Frost explains the importance of being decisive and taking business risks and coping even when you have little control over the circumstances – the circumstances? They were war…

Regulations and laws are one area that if not followed correctly can turn into a calamity. In **"Legal liabilities"** John Hardwick shares his advice, with hindsight, that small businesses should seek advice as early as possible if there is a legal problem looming, and to take as many precautions as possible to avoid the problem getting worse.

Going into business with family members can be fraught for many reasons. In chapter five, **"Family Matters"** Ralph Followell shares his experience of what happened to his dental practice when he was forced to leave his premises. He learnt about the importance of firming up on agreements and expecting the unexpected.

Not all calamities are reserved for commercial business. A Rotarian's surprise at finding out that the national charity he had just joined as an executive member was on the brink of becoming bankrupt despite what looked like a healthy cash balance, is told in **"Charities; cash counts"**. The special ending in this tale results in the award of the Paul Harris Fellowship Medal.

"Overblown" is a story about how a pharmacy picked up a sideline selling wheelchairs that nearly destroyed the business. John Vooght shares his lessons about sticking to the knitting, knowing when to let go and the appreciation that sometimes competition is a good thing.

The mystery "Mr X" describes how he felt when he discovered a chisel was on the loose in a prison in **"A "locky" business"**. Here the lessons were to focus on the small issues, vigilance and the importance of quick and focused action.

Roger Simmons experienced redundancy at an awkward age, forty-eight, and he shares his reflections on how he coped with it in **"Gaining from losing"** in chapter 9. He encountered ageism and went through the modern process of downshifting.

"Risky business" takes us into health care again, with Dr Helen Falcon reflecting on what she learnt when a bottle of water was accidentally replaced by something a lot more harmful. She learnt about the importance of listening and feedback, the necessity of fixing what can be fixed and to recognise the limitations of formal controls.

Finding the root cause of a calamity can be tricky and in chapter 11, **"Spilt milk"**, Des Brazier explains what happened when some foul smelling milk turned up at his processing plant and how they went about working out what had gone wrong.

"**In the public eye**" is a story about the difficulties of working for local government where all the business has to be conducted in public. Roy Collis explains what he encountered when presenting for modernising the County library services.

The death of a colleague and friend is one of the most significant calamities. In "**The importance of pause**", John Guest reflects on the events leading up to the death and his own role in it and how he coped. This chapter reviews the topic of stress and its impact.

Ian Bond brings this book to a conclusion with a short and lighthearted story called "**Rain or Shine**". We learn here about the importance of being prepared, especially for inclement weather, and the usefulness of humour as a means of coping with calamity.

As this book unfolded some themes came to light as common amongst all those who shared their stories. It seemed that it was easier to share the stories and reflect on them as time had passed. The more recent the event, the less easy it was to contemplate what happened and to identify the lessons. As a result, many of the stories in this book date back to earlier days in the careers of those who provided them.

It appears as though most of the calamities had an '*escalation*' effect. Whilst each one was in its own right an adverse event, most of them, if not nipped in the bud, would have become even worse. The *speed of reaction* to a crisis differed significantly according to the context and circumstance, as well as personal preference. Some individuals suggested that unless they had made a very speedy response they would have been worse off. In contrast, others said it was important to move slowly and not make any rash decisions.

All the contributors to stories in this book are characterised by an element of personal grit. Stepping up and sharing a personal and very real calamity to a world-wide audience is not to be under-estimated. It has taken them commitment, courage and humility – in themselves, all great characteristics of leaders who survive calamities.

Notes:
Each chapter ends with some notes for further reading. Many of these include Internet websites. These were correct at the time of publication though there is no guarantee they will continue in the form initially researched for this book.

Chapter 1

"Small things matter"

"Experience is the toughest teacher because she gives the test first, and then the lesson."

Unknown

Introduction

In any people orientated organisation, mistakes and accidents will be an emotive business, none more so than in health care. The story in this chapter is one that many healthcare workers will recognise and the principles easily transfer to other sectors. It is about how one small incident led to a fairly complex set of circumstances that needed resolving.

Key themes

Small things can have a huge impact

When we think of calamities and disaster we tend to remember the big events, the earthquakes, the collapse of large companies, the explosions and the deaths. However, many smaller difficulties are experienced every day and some of these can have significant consequences on individuals and their families. It is easy to overlook the smaller mistakes without understanding their true operational, emotional and financial impact. In this chapter, Dr Roger Bodley, a consultant radiologist, shares his story about how a cleaner came to be pricked by a dirty needle, and the impact of this incident.

Inspections and protocols can reduce error rates, but not avoid them entirely

Like many large and complex organisations, hospitals have many protocols and procedures designed to make the process of care and the patient's experience less variable and safer. Designing safety into organisation systems that depend significantly on human decision-making means that there will always be a higher potential for error than when working with mechanical systems. Humans are fallible – we all make mistakes, and there are many reasons why this happens. No matter how detailed the protocol and directions, there will always be room for error if a human is involved.

To tell or not to tell

In busy and pressurised organisations it is easy to overlook the small incidents. This can happen subconsciously – we might not even notice the little event – or consciously – we make the decision to ignore what happened and not to report it. If the incident is a big one, then taking no notice is difficult. The problem with small events is that they are easier to ignore. The big problem is that we know that many small events are precursors to the big one – ignore them at your peril.

Personal experience

Dr Roger Bodley is a consultant radiologist at Stoke Mandeville Hospital in England. This is a rural district general hospital with a world-renowned spinal injuries centre.

Roger trained as a student and junior doctor at Oxford, England and then practised as a general practitioner for six years in Australia. He returned to the UK in the mid-1980s and trained in radiology. He specialises in interventional "keyhole" procedures.

He does not hold a formal management position but believes that leadership is a factor in all jobs, at all levels.

"I had always considered myself obsessive about the handling of used needles and sharp objects after surgical procedures and I take great care to dispose of them promptly and properly. So I felt awful when it appeared I was probably responsible for one of our cleaners being accidentally pricked by a needle when she was clearing away clinical waste. Needles should be disposed of into a special plastic *sharps* bin so this kind of accident can't happen.

On a Monday afternoon I was carrying out a biopsy on the liver of someone who was jaundiced. This involves using a long needle for the biopsy and a small one to deliver a little bit of anaesthetic. It seems the small needle, which is transparent and nearly invisible, ended up in the clinical waste bag. Not surprisingly, the longer needle, which was more visible, and everything else was disposed of correctly.

The first I knew about a problem was when the head of our department told me the next day. Apparently the cleaner felt the prick of a needle on one of her fingers when she cleared away the waste bin during the evening. She reported it to her manager, who then reported it to the duty nurse, who filled out an accident report.

As it was possible that the needle could have come from a number of interventions carried out in the same treatment room on the Monday, I did think for a moment that it couldn't be mine so why should I have to deal with it. I couldn't believe it really was my fault as I was the one person who always nagged others about safety and took so much trouble over clearing up after myself.

However, I realised that the most important thing was to sort out the problem, and to learn from what happened. The sorting out took up a whole afternoon during which all routine work had to be postponed to the evening. I didn't begrudge this, but the impact of recovering from an accident is always far more effort than the preventative work. I think sometimes we don't report near misses and small incidents because we worry we will not have time to sort them out.

Why are needle stick injuries so important? Well, the obvious problem is that the needle will be contaminated in some way and it's possible for some diseases such as hepatitis and the HIV virus to be unintentionally transmitted to the person who is stuck by the needle. The cleaner needed to be offered some tests and I also had to contact the patient to ask him whether he would undergo similar tests. All of this was a needless worry for both the cleaner and the patient.

I rang the patient and asked him to come in for some blood tests but didn't explain fully why until I saw him. I felt it would be better to explain what happened face to face. He was not best pleased. At the time of this incident HIV was in the press a lot and there were many negative connotations with just having the test. He could have refused but in the end he agreed it was in the best interests of the cleaner and himself too. I did apologise to him and he accepted this was an unintentional error.

The cleaner was very anxious, as she knew the risks. She was keen to have the tests. I spent some time counselling her about what happened, as it was important we didn't lose her trust in us. She was an important member of our team and we relied on her to keep our treatment rooms to a high standard of cleanliness and she had a right to expect we would ensure her safety at all times.

In the end, the tests all proved negative, though this didn't mean there was no impact on the cleaner or the patient. The emotional upset and decision-making that had to be done was significant. Similarly, I felt shaken by the fact that I had made a mistake, even when I prided myself on being so careful. It seems that no matter what the protocols are, no matter how much training, no matter how many times I check, there is always room for a mistake to slip in. The danger seems to be in the routine and small things which are easy to forget about.

Reports indicate that around 1 million needle stick injuries happen per year in the USA. In the 1980s at least 50,000 to 60,000 health workers contracted serious infections from needle sticks, with around 200–300 deaths per year.

There are more than 20 different diseases that can be transmitted; for example, hepatitis, HIV, syphilis, malaria, tuberculosis, herpes and others.

The cost of testing, treatment, counselling, medical costs and lost wages is put at between $200 and $2,000 if the person is not infected, and if they are infected with, for example HIV, the costs rise to $500,000 through to $1,000,000.

(Source: Deadly Needles, San Francisco Chronicle: 13–15 April 1998)

In the UK it is estimated there may be 500,000 needle sticks per year. The UK tends to focus on the responsibility of the individual and the use of special bins to place needles in, while the emphasis to improve safety in the USA is on the design of safer needle devices.

(Source: *Nursing Times*, 26 Feb 99)

As a result of this, and other similar incidents, the hospital introduced a policy where anyone who experiences this sort of problem goes immediately to the emergency department where they receive certain immunisations as an immediate precaution, and also receive early counselling. I think there are a lot less incidents now.

This accident happened quite a while ago and in telling the story for this book I spent some time reviewing my own practice with regards used needles. I was astonished to find that when I thought about it, I discovered some potential problems and near misses. It was a bit like taking your driving test when you've been driving for twenty years – somehow the bad habits creep in and become so intuitive that it is difficult to even notice them, let alone stop them!

Leadership reflections

This story about a needle stick injury highlights a number of key issues for leaders:

- Taking ownership
- Making the apology
- Reporting near misses
- Understanding human fallibility
- Ensuring a supportive learning culture

Taking ownership

Things will go wrong and it is so easy to ignore the little events or try to blame someone else for the bigger ones. It is also easy to spend a lot of time working out who is to blame and therefore who should sort out the problem. However, sometimes, the most important task is to recover from the calamity – especially when other people, such as patients, customers, suppliers, contractors, staff etc. are involved and potentially badly affected.

One way of looking at calamities is to see the wider picture of what happened. In many cases there is not one person who is to blame, but rather a whole series of events that are all connected in one complicated web of interactions.

It is important to appreciate the complexities of how chains of events come about. An essential leadership role is to ensure those adversely affected by an incident, no matter how big or small, are taken care of in a timely and appropriate manner.

Do you think there is a culture of blame in your team or organisation? What do you think you could do to help break this down?

In what ways can you lead by example by not blaming someone, but immediately getting on and resolving the issue?

Making the apology

Patients, customers and others who are on the receiving end of something going wrong, usually say when they make their complaint that all they are really looking for is an apology. They would like the doctor, the company or the supplier, to acknowledge they have made a mistake, and then, and only then, can both parties move on in their relationship. Some of those impacted will take the issue further and may sue for compensation; others may feel the apology is sufficient. However, for many, the complaints journey is a complex and emotive one that often ends up in court or at a tribunal, just because someone couldn't say sorry.

"Recommendation 34

When things go wrong, patients are entitled to receive an acknowledgement, an explanation and an apology."

Learning from Bristol: The NHS Department of Health Response to the Report of the Public Inquiry into children's heart surgery at the Bristol Royal Infirmary 1984–1995

(http://www.doh.gov.uk/bristolinquiryresponse/bristolresponsech2.htm)

When last did you make an apology for something that went wrong, even if it was not directly your fault?

Can you think of occasions when an apology would have made the situation better?

Reporting near misses

For every accident that happens, research indicates that there were a possible 300 times when the incident nearly happened. This is known as the Heinrich Ratio: 300 – 29 –1 ratio between near misses, minor injuries and major injuries. Heinrich also estimated that 88% of all near misses and workplace injuries resulted from unsafe acts.

Many organisations, including hospitals, have systems in place to record and analyse adverse incidents. Some of these also capture information on near misses. The reward for focusing on near misses is the knowledge that you can avoid an incident happening – take evasive action before something goes wrong. Many staff will prefer the more positive process of looking for patterns and taking preventative action, than going through the process of reviewing processes that have gone wrong.

One of the problems with near misses is that we become so used to the routines we carry out that we no longer spot the risks. Think about driving your car down a narrow lane. You might be travelling

"The eye sees a great many things, but the average brain records very few of them."

Thomas Elva Edison

5

at 50 mph and coming towards you is another car travelling at the same speed. You pass safely. However, there may have been only two inches between your wing mirrors; two inches apart from a devastating 100 mph impact. You may experience this every day as you travel to and from work. Maybe once a year you experience the snap of mirrors as they brush against one another – a near miss to remind you of the risks. Or maybe you didn't get that warning…

The theory suggests that for every reported needle stick incident, there were approximately 300 occasions when an incident nearly happened. For Roger this means there were plenty of times when he nearly forgot to put the needle in the sharps bin, but remembered at the last moment. Obviously it is not possible to attend to all the potential problems all the time – we would never get any work done. To survive we filter out many of the cues and signals sent to our brain, and this is part of the problem – our inbuilt potential for error – our human fallibility.

> Recall the last time you were involved in or responsible for an adverse event.
>
> Can you think of any occasions before it happened where there were warning signs?
>
> What were these?
>
> Have you noticed any near misses since the event happened?
>
> On what areas could you focus your attention and try to identify near misses so you can avoid a potential accident?
>
> If you can't recall a near miss, are you satisfied with your ability to notice the small warnings that could signal a drift towards a larger calamity?

Understanding human fallibility

"The only consistent people are the dead."

Aldous Huxley

We are not perfect and we will always make mistakes. The number of mistakes we make every working day is potentially large. If no major untoward incident happens we may not notice just how many mistakes we are making. We are limited by the way in which our senses and brain works. Some of us have in-built biases that affect how we work. For example, have you ever put the cat in the fridge and the milk outside the back door? Or closed the front door behind you to find you've walked out without your keys? Or forgotten your home phone number? These are all instances of cognitive confusion.

We can make errors because we miss something inadvertently (an interruption diverts our attention), we select the wrong information (look at what is in the sharps bin but not look at the treatment table to see what is left behind), ignore information that is available, and have over confidence in our abilities (don't see the needle because we don't usually forget to dispose of it appropriately).

What do you think are the most common types of errors that you make?

Do you miss out things because your attention is distracted or do you actually make the mistake because you are concentrating too much?

In what way can your personal errors affect your business?

What plans can you put in place to minimise the impact of these personal mishaps?

Ensuring a supportive learning culture

A key factor in being able to cope with large and small mistakes is to have a trusting work environment. This means feeling comfortable owning up to your own mistakes and helping others review theirs in a constructive way. It helps when the people you work with have the same co-operative work ethic and are personable and friendly. Roger Bodley suggested the most important factor when dealing with calamities at work was to have good relationships in place – without them, it would not be possible to learn from mistakes.

In what way is your work environment conducive to the reporting and constructive discussion of errors?

What can you, as a leader, do to support the development of appropriate working relationships?

Conclusion

Small mistakes will happen. Whether these grow into large calamities that have a severe impact on the individuals involved and the organisation, is largely down to the ability of leaders; the ability to recognise mistakes as learning opportunities, the ability to appreciate the potential impact of near misses and small adverse events, and the ability to enable a supportive culture based on good working relationships.

Annotated bibliography and references

Interested in learning more about **patient safety**? There are numerous sites on the internet that cover this issue. Many hospitals will have their own site with guidelines and statistics. Check out the UK NHS National Patient Safety Agency www.npsa.nhs.uk. An excellent source of information and links to health care safety and improvement tools and techniques is the website co-owned by the British Medical Journal and the

Institute of Healthcare Improvement in Boston – www.qualityhealthcare.org

Near misses are well known in the safety world. Any search engine will generate useful papers and articles, specially if you search using keywords from your own industry e.g. "*near+miss hotel*".

The Heinrich ratio: in Heinrich, H.W. 1941. *Industrial Accident Prevention*. 2nd edition, McGraw Hill, New York, NY.

Most of the work on **human fallibility,** as related to accidents, originated with the airline industry. Searches using the terms *human fallibility* and *human factors*, will elicit a wide variety of material.

Chapter 2

"Rallying round"

"No pessimist ever discovered the secrets of the stars, or sailed to an uncharted land, or opened a new heaven to the human spirit."

Helen Keller

Introduction

Fire is devastating. It not only destroys buildings, company assets, personal belongings and precious mementoes, it also has the potential for emotional and psychological damage. In this chapter, Desmond May recalls the time when part of the school where he was headmaster burnt down, and shares his experiences and lessons learned.

Key themes

The show must go on

When calamities befall us it is easy to submit to their pressure and perhaps wallow in the agony of the circumstances. For some businesses and institutions the option of closing down while the issues are resolved may not be an option.

Calamities can bring out the best in people

It is well known that problems and disasters can unite disparate groups of people. New alliances, relationships and friendships are often borne out of a crisis. Individuals also come to the fore and do things you'd never expect.

Contingency plans are important

There are two parts to contingency plans; preparing for and preventing a calamity, and plans to cope and recover. In the instance of this school, there were many preventative activities and plans in place; however, none could cope with the unexpected event of a drug addict trying to burn down all the buildings. The lesson learnt from this experience was the need to draw on all possible resources in the recovery and rebuilding period.

Personal experience

Desmond May was born and educated in Sheffield, UK. He trained as a teacher and progressed from assistant teacher, to head of modern languages, to deputy head and finally Headmaster.

In a career spanning 40 years he covered only four schools, 25 of these years at the school where he was to become Headmaster – Sir Henry Floyd Grammar School in Aylesbury.

For Des, the concept of leadership is defined by the ability to take command of responsibility when necessary and to encourage people to give of their best, whatever their skills and opportunity.

The Arson Prevention Bureau reported that in 1996 there were 1,400 arson attacks on schools in the UK. They believe this figure is increasing.

The costs in 1996 were estimated to be in the region of £50 million – and that is not counting the emotional cost involved.

They suggested that installing better lighting, surveillance cameras and fences could prevent some incidents.

(Source: BBC News 30 June 1998)

"There are very few happenings that can halt the delivery of education to the pupils at a mixed grammar school in Aylesbury, but a raging fire is as close as you can get. On the evening of Saturday, October 29th, 1983, the Sir Henry Floyd Grammar School had its main hall, dining room and kitchen completely destroyed by an arsonist who later blamed his drug habit for his actions. The financial cost reached nearly half a million pounds.

My deputy and I, having been alerted by the Chief Education Officer, Roy (now Sir Roy) Harding, were faced with such a scene of devastation that it led to one of his staff asking if the school would be able to open on the following Monday, after half-term. I was quite amazed that anyone could even think that way, knowing the quality and calibre of both students and staff, so I replied somewhat abruptly that it would take more than a fire to close us down. As far as I was concerned there was no option but to keep the school open.

My initial enthusiasm palled a bit when I worked out the implications of my ambition. As we held regular religious school assemblies we needed a replacement gathering place. Importantly, many of our students travelled a long distance to and from school and we needed to be able to provide them with a hot meal at lunchtime. Also, the geography department had lost all of its books, maps and records and whilst this meant some of the students revelled in the loss of a few test papers, an entire department needed to be replaced.

But, says the management manual, all challenges are opportunities, so we set to work to tackle the major problems.

Fortunately the fire was at the weekend and there were no injuries to any pupils or staff members. These school fires are becoming more common nowadays, mostly started by pupils or ex-pupils of the school over the weekend or during school holidays.

First of all, I called in all outstanding favours from my next door neighbour, Peter Gibson, who willingly sacrificed his College's keep fit classes to hand over their main hall. This covered not only our regular morning assemblies, but also our many evening functions like "A" level presentation evening.

Secondly, the local authority agreed to put a temporary cabin on our croquet lawn in front of my office – much to the chagrin of our senior master who was concerned about the loss of the use of an important sporting facility! However, we needed somewhere for our pupils to eat; in the few weeks it took to get the facility installed, they had been served only hot soup in the foyer of one of the buildings.

Finally, my colleagues in other local schools elsewhere in the county rallied round with books and equipment and we received support from the county's educational supplies department.

The most important factor, however, was the support I received from the staff and students. They cheerfully put up with the dust, chaos, cramped conditions and improvisations I had to impose on them during the several months it took to replace the buildings. Not a single day's teaching was lost during this time!

Sir Henry Floyd Grammar School began as the Aylesbury Technicon and moved to its present site in the 1950s. It has over 1000 pupils and is now a specialist performing arts centre. In 1993 it was named as an "outstandingly successful school" in an OFSTED report.

They also enthusiastically helped the School's Parents' Society with its fundraising efforts under the soubriquet of the Phoenix Fund; they arranged a fashion show compered by a TV celebrity, Noel Edmunds, and a Gala dinner with John Junkin, TV actor and script writer, as our after-dinner speaker. Their activities raised several thousand pounds that went towards classroom and laboratory fittings and equipment, as well as textbooks.

When the site had been cleared and the rebuilding started, I have to admit there was a feeling of deflation among all the members of the school, including me. Perhaps the adrenaline had carried us through, and my hardest task was to restore morale after the experience of us all being companions in adversity. From feeling superior, we went back to being ordinary mortals still worrying about the more mundane if necessary tasks in school – but I believe we all benefited from the experience!"

Leadership reflections

In this story, Desmond May highlights a number of leadership concerns – both during and after the crisis

- Never giving up
- Creativity in adversity
- Capitalising on connections and relationships
- Contingency planning

Never giving up

A critical leadership capability is to be able to discern when the calamity is such that it is best to walk away and start afresh, or whether to dig in and muster all your energies, and those of your staff, to recover from the problem.

As seen in this example, this decision is unlikely to be one where there are board papers, analyses and much discussion. In this case, it was an autocratic decision taken by the leader with strength and courage. It is in difficult times that followers look to their leaders for direction and inspiration. Maybe this calls for a period of reflection – maybe it suggests immediate action; what matters is the leader's ability to grasp the situation and provide a sense of direction.

In this story, the headmaster gave his staff, students and parents a positive sense of ownership of the solution to the problem. Their energies were directed in a constructive way.

Have you ever been called upon to make a split second decision about whether to continue an operation and put temporary plans in place, or whether to stop the process and buy time to fix the problem?

If you have, do you think you made the most appropriate decision?

If you haven't, can you visualise and feel what it would be like to be on the spot and under pressure?

Creativity in adversity

The chaotic time between something ending (such as the loss of the building in the fire) and the new beginning (such as moving into a new building) is a time well known for its creativity. William Bridges called this the '*neutral zone*'. He suggests this is a risky time when priorities get confused, anxiety increases, miscommunication is rife and systems become unreliable.

The key objectives for any leader who experiences this 'neutral zone' are to get his team through in one piece and to capitalise on the creative possibilities. To survive this difficult time, Bridges advises:

- *Putting temporary structures and policies into place*; using the foyer as a canteen
- *Helping people understand what happened*; spending time listening to concerns, allaying fears and explaining what has happened as well as what has not happened
- *Ensuring everyone is kept well informed with progress;* holding regular staff meetings and providing information to parents
- *Developing new teams by bringing people together who may not have*

worked together before. For example, teaching staff, county architects department and maintenance supervisors all worked together to find ways to keep the school open

- *Schedule time-out for reflection and discussion;* senior staff met together away from the school to discuss emerging problems and their solutions
- *Encourage experimentation;* the fire at school enabled new building designs to be created – for example, ensuring classrooms and science laboratories were more flexible in their design so they could be used for different disciplines. Also the assembly hall platform was no longer fixed and stage lighting completely changed to suit school dramatic productions.

> What creative solutions and initiatives have you come up with when in the midst of a crisis?
>
> What needs to happen in your workplace to create the tension for creative change?
>
> If you are currently experiencing a crisis at work, what action can you take to help your staff and teams make sense of the difficulties and changes?
>
> To what extent do you schedule time for personal and team reflection?

Capitalising on connections and relationships

Some leaders cope with their role by working alone, as distinct and singular commanders of their 'ship'. This is an option that may deliver good business results; however, in times of hardship and calamity, support from other individuals and organisations may be crucial. The isolated leader can find themselves with no-one to turn to for advice or practical support.

Most of the Grammar School Head's colleagues sent financial contributions, textbooks and equipment to replace those damaged by the fire – often without being asked.

Some of the connections and relationships may be less obvious and in a crisis some positive unexpected things can happen. For example,

- one of the pupils from this school was at a party when he heard the arsonist offer to burn the school down so that one of the girls wouldn't need to come back after half term. The pupil cycled six miles to raise the alarm with the police
- a member of staff offered to convert workshop benches into desks
- the School's Parents' Society Committee was in touch on the first Monday after the fire to say they had decided to form the Phoenix Fund

Think back to a crisis you have experienced; who was on hand to help you?

What are your key networks and contacts?

Who can you call on and rely upon in a crisis?

Can you recall a time when you have helped a colleague in a crisis? Perhaps there have been times when you could have helped but didn't? What will you do in future?

Contingency planning

No amount of fire drills, fire extinguishers, sprinklers and alarms can anticipate a drug addict breaking widows, using a Molotov cocktail or pushing flaming cardboard onto curtains – causing a major fire. However, as fires become a depressingly increasing feature of school life, as a precautionary measure more security and better lighting is being introduced onto most premises.

Large international companies usually have contingency plans where they can hire new buildings with communication and computing facilities and move their staff in so they can carry on working if their head office is out of action. For smaller businesses and public services such as schools and hospitals this is seldom an option.

Scenario planning is one way for leaders and their top teams to think through what they would do in a crisis. Whilst these scenarios will probably never cover the unexpected event that does happen, the process of thinking through the alternatives is a helpful one; both psychologically as well as practically.

After the fire at the Sir Henry Floyd Grammar School, where possible, rebuilding was done with flexibility in mind – where classrooms could be dual purpose. They looked to 'future-proof' the school as well as provide flexibility in the event of a similar incident. Also, more detailed plans have been written up on ways to cope with something similar happening again, and ways to keep the school open, no matter what the calamity.

If you lost your office to fire tomorrow – what would be your contingency plan?

What preparations can you make in advance that would cost very little now but would make a big difference in the event of an unexpected crisis?

What preventative steps are you taking to avoid a crisis (for example virus checking your computers, flood protection and insurance, theft and personal safety of staff)?

Commentary

By Sir Roy Harding

"As the Chief Education Officer, I would be told of any important incident in which the police or fire service were involved. Part of my responsibilities involved the appropriate education of over 100,000 school children in more than 350 schools. Considerable delegation was inevitable. We had a system which we hoped would be effective if, for example, a Head suddenly died on a school site because of an accident or a heart attack – both happened – or a school was wholly or partly destroyed by fire. In this case I knew that the Head was very capable. I knew too that those clearing the site and designing the new buildings as well as those handling tenders for construction would cope with any problems and help with solutions.

At the time of the fire, Des May was a well-established headmaster who had welded the school teaching and non-teaching staff into a good team. He had very good relationships with his governors, parents and staff of the local education authority.

He was surprised that one of my staff would question whether the school would open on the Monday. Well, he wouldn't have known that in similar circumstances many other heads would have said 'no', or perhaps have given a conditional 'yes'. This is not surprising as most Heads were selected for their educational experience and philosophy, and their evidence of ability to select and motivate staff, rather than their potential to deal with any crisis.

In the case of this crisis at the Sir Henry Floyd Grammar School there was no need to bring in external help to overcome any immediate difficulty. The issues were handled promptly and professionally by the team at the school.

In Des May's 'Personal Experience' as shared in this chapter, I think the key successes seem to lie in the background of the long-term creation of good associations and relationships. Capitalising on connections and the opportunity for creativity in adversity are inevitably easier when rallying round is badly needed.

Conclusion

By definition, calamities are unexpected and often at times painful events that impact many people. Different leaders respond differently in different situations. What matters is the appropriateness of the response and, in the example of Des May, the ability to draw on resources and relationships not only to keep the business running, but also to capitalise on the creative opportunities that change can bring.

Annotated bibliography and references

William Bridges (1998) *Managing Transitions; making the most of change.*
Nicholas Brearley: UK

> Practical advice on how to deal with change, both planned and
> unplanned. Introduces the idea of there being an ending of the old
> way, then the confusion of the neutral zone, followed by a new
> beginning. Excellent and helpful guide to a difficult subject.

www.continencyplanning.com

> A comprehensive site with an extensive knowledge base. Useful articles
> and advice on searchable topics.

www.contingency-planning-disaster-recovery-guide.co.uk

> Excellent guide, especially relevant for small businesses. Covers starting
> point, impact assessment, the plan, testing, awareness and
> maintenance.

Chapter 3

"Big events, big decisions"

"If there was a simple formula for success and it was easy to follow, everybody would be doing it."

Edward C Johnson III

Introduction

Wars are events that happen to other people. However, the conflagrations that happen in various parts of the world can have a direct impact on your local community – and this means an impact on your local business. There are approximately 26 million motor vehicles in the UK and this means they need to have access to fuel. So what happens when a major source of petrol and diesel, the Middle East, goes to war?

This chapter is a story about how James Frost, then Joint Chief Executive of a group of petrol filling stations throughout the UK survived the effects of two Middle Eastern wars and the resulting oil crises in the UK.

Key themes

Being decisive

Real crises always seem to happen when resources are low (in this case the only other executive board member was in South America and uncontactable) or – whenever you are least likely expect them. A critical leadership competency is the ability to take responsibility for making a decision, whether large or small. During a crisis, there may not be the luxury of time to perform long-winded analyses and discussion. Decisions need to be made taking a pragmatic assessment of the problem – and quickly.

Taking risks

There are two different extremes of coping behaviour for a senior leader to use when a significant organisational calamity happens:

1. Wait and see, soften the blow; tentatively ride out the storm
2. Decide, *now*, how to react; take radical measures to ensure organisational survival

Every business and every circumstance is different. Leaders need to be able to work out which option is appropriate for the issue at hand.

Coping when you have little control over the circumstances

What sets this story aside from many others in this book is the wider context of crises happening outside the industry and even outside the country. Whilst wars are, fortunately, not that common, similar issues can occur when you and your business are impacted by situations outside your direct control. For example, when the drivers of a wholesaler's delivery fleet go on strike, your corner shop may find its regular source of product unavailable. Or if a regulatory body grounds a certain type of cargo aircraft, you may find you've lost the most efficient and effective means of transporting your perishable products.

Learning lessons

The current trend of senior managers and leaders in large organisations moving positions every two to three years, has some advantages in exposing them to developmental experiences, however, there are also some distinct disadvantages. If events do repeat themselves, then senior leaders who are still in place who experienced something similar, will benefit their organisations. For example, the impact of the Iran-Iraq war in 1979/80 on retail fuel supplies in the UK was very similar to what happened during the Yom Kippur War of 1973. Being able to transfer the lessons learnt from one experience to the other helped James Frost's business survive the calamities and to profit from them.

Personal experience

"With the outbreak of the Yom Kippur war, the OPEC countries caused the price of crude oil to quadruple, by reducing supply, forcing the British Government to introduce a form of rationing of motor fuel by way of allocations of fuel to service station forecourts and hence pump prices to rocket upwards. Within 24 hours I had to make two thirds of our 250 staff redundant from our twenty-five petrol stations at our company Look Petroleum Ltd. The 25 petrol stations were owned and supplied by 8 different oil company suppliers. At the time most of these staff were on hourly contracts and I worked with my managers to implement the redundancy process. We also asked the remaining staff to undertake different jobs, so all service station managers, for example, also filled the role of forecourt cashier.

This redundancy process was very stressful, all the more for having to take the decision on my own. However, there was an urgency to save the company and at least keep it going for the remaining staff. It was an unpleasant decision to have to take and implement but it was the only way we were going to survive.

I also took the decision to move immediately from a 24-hour operation to only 10-hours per day to cut both staffing and electricity costs. After wages, electricity was our highest overhead, hence the benefit in reducing opening hours to daylight hours only.

It was a drastic cost-cutting exercise, but I had worked out the figures and they showed that the potential impact on turnover, of fuel shortages and rationing, would mean the company would not survive if the current levels of overhead remained. As a small company we did not have the financial reserves or ability that the larger oil companies had to sustain large financial losses.

These immediate decisions turned out to be critical for the company. At the time the UK was dependent on Middle Eastern crude oil, so when OPEC quadrupled the price of crude the economic impact for the country was instant and severe. The UK Government quickly instituted rationing of the supply of fuel to oil companies and therefore to petrol stations. This was a complex process that meant we often only knew about our quota for the week when we had already sold it! However, we soon learnt to predict and second-guess the rationing amounts and then adjust our operation to match the supply we were given. This meant we also increased the price of the fuel to the customer at the pump. This went some way to reducing panic buying though we still had customers queuing to buy very

James Frost started off business life as an accountant. His diverse career has seen him managing different types of businesses at the same time; he spent 34 years in the petroleum industry, a total of 21 years in banking and fund management, and 27 years in property management, where he is still active.

He has experience of working in both publicly listed companies and private family companies.

OPEC stand for "Organisation of Petroleum Exporting Countries". It is currently made up of: 7 countries from the Middle East (Algeria, Iran, Kuwait, Libya, Saudi Arabia, Qatar and United Arab Emirates) plus Indonesia, Nigeria and Venezuela. Iraq is currently no longer a member but clearly has an influence in the region and was a founding member in 1960. They act as a cartel and that is why they can have such an influence.

OPEC currently accounts for about 37% of world oil production and if you include Iraq at its pre Gulf War quota of 3.2m barrels a day the percentage shoots up to about 42%. At the time of the 1973 war the percentage was very much higher because there was so little oil being produced from the North Sea and elsewhere.

small amounts. Eventually the Government intervened and the retail price was capped.

In early 1974 rationing ended and operations returned to a new normal. We had to re-employ new staff and re-open the longer hours. This itself was a challenging exercise. However, this was then followed by a vicious price war amongst the oil companies as they tried to recover turnover lost through rationing. Look Petroleum Ltd competed on price, with the aid of oil company subsidies, as the oil companies owned the sites and wanted to protect their assets that were valued according to volume of fuel sold.

In 1979–80 I had the chance to revisit what I learnt earlier when Iraq invaded Iran. This time the government left the oil companies to organise allocations of fuel to forecourts. However, as before, motorists panicked, supply prices rose and the retail pump price escalated, similar to what happened in the Yom Kippur War in 1973–4.

By this time, Look Petroleum Ltd had grown from 25 oil company-owned petrol stations to 50 company-owned petrol stations. These were again mostly operated twenty-four hours a day with a complement of some 500 staff.

Now, as Chief Executive of the company, at the outbreak of war I asked myself three questions:

(a) What actions did we take last time and were they the right ones?
(b) What happened afterwards, and could that happen again?
(c) Would I do anything differently, knowing what I know now?"

I focused a lot of my attention on what would happen after the war ended and normal supplies were resumed. After all, there is no point in working to outlast the crisis only to find that the company doesn't survive if there is an ensuing price war! This time round we owned the petrol stations so the oil company suppliers had a lesser interest in giving support, at their cost, if a price war did in fact ensue.

Following some scenario planning where I assessed supply, sales, price, profit and cash flow, I ended up taking similar, but watered down, actions to last time. I cut operating hours to 16 hours per day, rather than 10 hours per day. We also reduced the amount of fuel each customer could buy at each visit so as to make supplies of fuel last the extra hours. This meant that the forecourt shops remained open longer for the sale of higher margin goods.

It certainly helped that I had experienced the first war six years earlier. Whilst it would have been possible to write down some of what happened and how it was dealt with, codified knowledge is never the same as the real experience. Not least because it lacks gut feel and instinct. Both these events were big issues for the Company.

I learnt that survival is about being decisive and having the courage to carry out difficult decisions. It worked. At the end of the Iran–Iraq war and before the inevitable price war started (as I expected it would once again to rebuild lost volumes), the business was sold – at five times what it was worth the year before the Iran–Iraq war started. We were an easy way of rebuilding a buying oil company's lost volume."

Have you ever been called upon to make a split second decision about whether to continue an operation and put temporary plans in place, or whether to stop the process and buy time to fix the problem?

If you have, do you think you made the most appropriate decision?

If you haven't, can you visualise and feel what it would be like to be on the spot and under pressure?

Assessing the risks

No business activity is risk free. A key role for senior leaders is to guide the organisation along a path that lies between bankruptcy due to too much caution, and bankruptcy due to taking too high a risk. This is an oscillating path with the organisation taking corrective turns as it progresses.

"You don't have guarantees in this world. You've got to take chances"

Muriel Siebert

Corporate attitude to risk

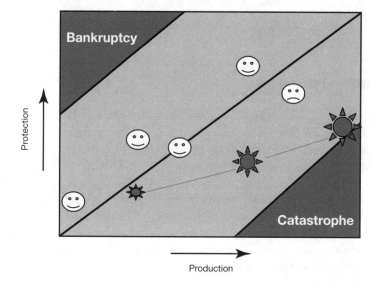

What is the most risky decision you've ever made in your business?

How did you arrive at that decision?

To what extent do you feel it was an appropriate decision?

What would you do differently in the future?

Knowing the business; understanding numbers

One of the advantages of leading a smallish organisation is it is easier to have a grasp on the detail of the business. For example, to have all the financial details to hand. This can help enormously when it comes to decision-making in a crisis. On the other hand, in large organisations, the financial details are often best known by the financial director and the chief executive may not be expected to know all of these without referring to others for advice.

Regardless of the size of organisation, in a time of crisis, the leader who has a good grasp of the economics of the business is better prepared and enabled to make decisions most appropriate to the survival of the business.

What are the key financial indicators in your business?

To what extent could you make a decision affecting the financial viability of your company – and make that decision now?

How much would you have to refer to others? To what extent would this be appropriate in a crisis?

Making decisions

If you're confident about what needs to be done then making the decision to progress is easier when you're on your own. Large organisations where there may be a number of committees involved in the decision-making process may take much longer to reach a conclusion.

In some cases committees may help to ensure a wider perspective is taken and the debate and analysis can avoid inappropriate decision-making. In contrast, there may be a situation where there is no time for such a lengthy process and survival depends on one person to take charge and initiate action.

	Committee/Group decision-making	Individual decision-making
Advantages	Wide perspective and different points of view	Single view so quicker time to reach decision Easier to explain the reasoning
Disadvantages	Need for discussion and possible consensus may take too long Large numbers of people involved does not necessarily avoid *group think* (the tendency to agree with each other even when inappropriate to do so)	Reflects only one point of view Potentially greater risk as something may be missed

Recall when you last made a decision (of any size and importance) on your own. In hindsight, was this an appropriate and effective decision?

What would you do differently in the future?

Applying experience

There is no substitute for experience. The current trends to extract and codify knowledge, gathering all the facts in the hope they will be useful to others, may sometimes be helpful. However, in the cut and thrust of business and leadership, the capability of the leader to cope personally and to guide their organisation through troubled times is of paramount importance.

When did you have to cope with something that was so unusual that you had no experience to rely on?

How did that feel?

To whom did you turn to for support?

Conclusion

Crises that impact your business can come from unexpected sources. Events in other countries or in organisations somehow connected to your business can have an enormous affect on your viability. Often these events are not ones for which you might have developed contingency plans. Because they are unexpected they may require urgent decision-making with radical changes implemented.

There is no one way to deal with any crisis. The capability of the senior leader to personally take responsibility for tough decisions and to carry out radical changes is critical.

Post script

A third Middle East War, also involving Iraq, took place in April 2003. Would you have conducted your operations differently? James Frost would.

Annotated bibliography and references

Michael Doyle (Foreword), Sam Kaner, Lenny Lind, Duane Berger, Catherine Toldi, Sarah Fisk (1996) *Facilitator's Guide to Participatory Decision Making.* New Society Publishers.
     This is an excellent resource for guiding group decision making.

http://www.mindtools.com/pages/main/newMN_TED.htm
     Mindtools have some good links to various decision-making techniques such as Pareto analysis, paired comparison analysis, grid analysis, decision trees, force field analysis, cost benefit analysis etc.

For further information about knowledge management then one of the best resources available on the web is http://www.brint.com/km/

Chapter 4

"Legal liabilities"

"Sometimes you win, sometimes you lose, sometimes you get rained out."

Satchel Paige III

Introduction

Whatever your business or your status you will nearly always need to employ someone – one exception may be if you're a sole trader. As soon as you do you take on legal responsibilities, these should never be underestimated.

This chapter is a short story about one of John Hardwick's experiences in dealing with employee contractual issues – where it went wrong, and what he learnt from the experience.

Key themes

Seek advice

Some issues, especially employment and personnel ones, require specialist advice. Seek it and use it.

Take precautions

Ending up in court is never the best option. Most crises can be resolved without recourse to legal procedures. Many can be avoided in the first place. When employee contracts are at issue, then it is always worthwhile seeking guidance from experts.

Personal experience

"She lost her baby just before it was due and wanted to come back to work. But by then I'd already started the redundancy process. We had

After graduating with a degree in Applied Chemistry, John spent seven years working on problems in the manufacture of photographic film. He then spent ten years involved in the manufacture of selenium photoconductors for the early generation of plain paper photocopiers, rising to the role of Managing Director, before deciding to become his own boss and starting a High Street Quick Print Franchise in partnership with his wife Christine. They have run this business for the past sixteen years during which time it has grown to be one of the most successful in the UK.

The cost of losing an employee, whatever the circumstances can run into thousands of pounds. Reports suggest an average of £3,500 is spent per vacancy on recruitment. Add to this training costs, interim support (most jobs take on average 10 weeks to fill) and other indirect costs, not paying attention to employee turnover can be bad for your bottom line. And of course, adding any tribunal award makes it even worse.

agreed that she could go on maternity leave but just after she left, the organisational structure changed and her job was no longer available. That was why she was made redundant.

It was a very emotional and difficult time, not least of which because she had lost her baby. The whole episode was also confused by the fact I had made a mistake in the letter terminating her contract. I had mixed up some dates and this was later to be part of the legal argument at the tribunal.

We went through a court process that lasted more than a month. The final result was I had to pay 50% of the amount awarded to our ex-employee.

We were quite a large organisation of which I was the general manager. During the whole process there was very little support from our head office human resources (HR) department. They were 30 miles away and seemed to me to be quite remote. After this experience the HR procedures were tightened and they became more involved with various local employee issues.

I was a member of a professional organisation that provided legal advice and this was immensely helpful and supportive. During the tribunal they organised for an expert to represent me.

What I learnt was to seek advice before getting involved with employee contractual issues. I also realised the benefit of being a member of a professional organisation and I have continued to make sure that I also contribute to these organisations. I think that legal issues are handled a lot better nowadays as there is a lot more attention paid to the detail and to the way that people are handled."

Who deals with the human resources issues in your organisation?

Do you feel remote locations are adequately supported?

To whom would you turn to for advice on how to handle a similar issue to the one in this story?

What benefits are available to you by being a member of an appropriate professional organisation?

Handling people when the structures change

Most people are not intrinsically motivated to sue their company if anything goes wrong. Although under the British Legal Aid system it may cost the ex-employee nothing to sue. It is therefore even more important to avoid such situations. Times of organisational change is when the probability of something going awry increases.

To get the best out of your staff, they need to feel safe and secure, know when and how they get paid. Any change in employment terms and conditions needs special attention, whether it is for one member of staff or the whole company. Managers are not expected to know all the ins and outs of employment law, and you need to get specialist advice, whether available from within your company or externally.

> Recall a time when you feel you didn't handle an employee issue as well as you might have.
>
> What could you have done to avoid any problems?
>
> From whom would you get legal advice?
>
> How would you pay for it?
>
> What will you now do in the future?

Coping with court procedures

One of the lessons John learnt was the importance of paying attention to detail; the small mistake about dates on the letters was a key factor in the court case. During the tribunal he had to pay equal attention to many small, but important details.

The law, for appropriate reasons, has some firm procedures that need to be followed. Getting the right advice is important. As John found out, court proceedings can take a long time and suck energy out of a small business. If you find yourself in a difficult legal position, then it is important to recognise that it will take both time and effort to resolve it. You may need to ensure you have appropriate support back in the business to cover you whilst you attend to the legalities.

> "Experience is the name everyone gives to their mistake."
>
> Oscar Wilde

> Recall an occasion where you were, or nearly were, embroiled in a legal issue.
>
> How did you or could you handle the time commitment of court proceedings?

Supporting remote locations

Do you work in the head office of a business that has a number of remote locations? How well are you supporting these locations through the core business processes of human resources, finance, research and development, as well as marketing and other centralised activities?

The tension between centralising and decentralising activities is always present in large organisations. The benefits, either way, are mixed:

The benefits of **centralisation** include:

- Greater control over strategy and operations
- Simpler control systems
- Easier allocation and optimisation of resources
- Quicker decision making

The disadvantages of centralisation include:

- Costly overheads
- Difficulty in responding to local needs

In comparison, **decentralisation**:

- Is best when the organisation is so large and complex that decision making needs to be dealt with more locally
- Can encourage creativity and empowerment

Though the problems that can occur include:
- The problem of defining roles and responsibilities
- Loss of common or corporate purpose and vision
- Delayed decision making
- Increased bureaucracy

When part of your business is remote from your head office then you need good feedback systems so both parties know what the other is doing and requires. Most often the communication processes are in one direction, from the central location to the remote location, with the minimum communication up the line, usually focused only on management reporting. Keeping in touch with people who are not in the head office is important. Finding ways to do this beyond the formal reporting structure is key.

How do you know what problems your remote locations are dealing with at the moment?

How much do tribunals and personnel complaints cost your company?

What crises can you recall where you could have provided more support from the central location that may have avoided a tribunal?

How can you increase the amount of informal contact you have between central and remote locations?

Conclusion

Large companies have whole departments of specialists focusing on the topic of human resources and all the legal requirements that may need to be in place. In John's case, like that of many small business owners, learning the legal lessons often come through tough experiences. However, people will always be a company's greatest asset, so when you next review your operations, check you are seeing them on the asset side of your business plan.

"Reflection is the opposite of blame."

Otto Scharmer

Annotated bibliography and references

The UK Department of Trade and Industry website http://www.dti.gov.uk/er/ has a whole section dedicated to employment relations. This is a very useful port of call for information on employment rules, rights and regulations.

The Business Link website www.businesslink.org is a good resource for small businesses and includes some useful factsheets and FAQs.

Chapter 5

"Family matters"

"Success isn't permanent and failure isn't fatal."

Mike Ditka

Introduction

The unexpected surprise of having notice serviced on your business premises is unpleasant even when it doesn't come from a member of your family. In this chapter, dentist Ralph Followell tells his story of how he recovered from this situation and what he learnt in the process.

Key themes

Firm up agreements

It's hard to imagine that after ten years or more of getting on with your business, you find that the contracts and agreements you had in place were insufficient to see you through some difficult challenges. Many family businesses often forget, or prefer not, to support good working relationships with legally binding contracts.

Expect the unexpected

No matter how secure and sustainable your business feels, all small businesses are susceptible to disruption from seemingly unpredictable events.

In this chapter, Ralph was surprised by a little known clause in a legal agreement that did not run in his favour. The likelihood of it becoming an issue was small though nonetheless the risk was there.

Partner up

Calamities feel worse when you're on your own. Times of crisis might just be the stimulus for you to network and connect with others in similar predicaments to your own. Even competitors can learn to work together and benefit from collective and collaborative strategies.

Personal experience

Ralph Followell qualified as a dental surgeon in 1959 and has worked in general dental practice in England since then. During his wide experience of dental affairs and politics, including 10 years of prison service, he has held numerous dental committee posts at local, regional and national levels.

Ralph retired from full time practice in 1992 and spends much of his time as an active member of his community which includes running several charities. For his Rotary Club he makes Carol Floats and runs the local Youth Speaks competition. He is the Vicechair of Governors of a Local School

"Being served nine months' notice to vacate my business premises where I had my dental practice for more than ten years. I had thought I was secure there and had another nine years to run on the lease and was protected by the Landlord & Tenant Act. What I hadn't realised was the law permitted my landlord, who was also a dentist, to serve notice on my lease if the property was to be knocked down and redeveloped for his own use.

What made this extra difficult was that my landlord was a close family member. I had no choice but to take legal action and to go for compensation, which I got, though it took a year in time and a significant amount of personal energy.

I felt anger and dismay at what happened. Especially as I not only lost the long-term lease but my landlord may have gained financially in the process by the way in which we split the patients between our practices.

My dental practice at the time covered 5,000 patients and I worked with an associate. On the one hand, being on my own meant it was easier to take decisions, on the other hand, I had no direct work colleague to support me through this difficult period, other than my wife Jackie who was, of course, very much involved. I had to take my energy away from patients to look for new premises. Eventually the right place came on the market though this needed planning permission. This took nearly six months to agree and then I had to develop the site to make the premises suitable.

What followed was interesting, as within a short period of time, many other dental practices in the town relocated to the same road. Far from being a competitive issue this turned out to be helpful as we found a way to work together and provide cover during periods of planned and unplanned absence from work.

This was a period of considerable personal learning. On the legal side I realised that the standard contracts provided by my professional association, were insufficient in content and detail to fully protect a practising dentist from unexpected though surely not unforeseen events. The poor standard of the contract propelled me into action and I spent time ensuring that others did not have to go through similar experiences to my own.

Another issue was my unpreparedness for the management side of the business and for coping with complex planning regulations and the like. I trained as a dentist and at the time all this happened my management skills were appropriate for running a practice but not for dealing with town councils etc. I learnt the hard way and I put back the experience from this episode into many years of local, regional and national committee work. Regionally I was involved in planning dental services for new developments like Milton Keynes, and nationally, I was responsible for terms and conditions of service and remuneration for all NHS dentists in the UK.

The impact of this calamity was not only on my business. It was also a family matter and one that has caused concern and angst for many years.

And the final straw? The site from where I was evicted – it has never been redeveloped!"

> **So how long do small businesses survive?**
>
> Some close down because they are taken over, or the owner retires, or they experience some form of calamity – most often a financial one. In the UK, the figures suggest around one third of small businesses survive, and that since 1993 there is a modest improvement in survival.
>
> (Source: Small Business Service, Feb 2003)

Firm up on agreements

Although he was dealing with a close family member, Ralph avoided the temptation to go into business without a contract. He just found out that the lease had a clause that enabled it to be terminated under some very specific arrangements.

Many family businesses start up and grow in an organic way. Many thus don't get round to working on the contractual needs of individuals and the business. It almost seems like a lack of trust in the family to even have a contract. On the contrary, it is often the close family relationships that can be at risk when linked to business relationships. Good contracts – and good relationships – can reduce that risk.

> Does your business rely on a family member?
>
> To what extent do you have contracts in place to ensure your business remains intact, even through a family dispute?

Expect the unexpected

Ralph thought his lease was secure under the Landlord & Tenant Act. It wasn't. Not only did he think his lease was good, he also relied on the fact that it was with a close family member.

Calamities are, by definition, unexpected. If we know something bad is going to happen then we usually have time to take evading action – no calamity.

Businesses that have been running on the same contracts for many years can fall into a false sense of security. We usually expect something to go wrong in the early days of a new business, not 10 years in.

A useful business practice is, each year, to take a couple of the basic contracts on which you rely and review them thoroughly. Don't assume they are up to date or in good working order. Think about some 'what if' circumstances. Ask some colleagues to question you about what are the most unlikely problems they could think might happen with the contract.

> When last were you surprised by a contract or business arrangement that didn't go as you expected?
>
> Could you have anticipated what might have happened?
>
> What deals do you have in a place that you feel are a dead cert; are they perfect? Now get out the contracts and review them, looking for how they might let you down.

Partner up

Coping with a crisis when your business is single-handed – just you – is no mean feat. Meeting with town planners, going to estate agents, meeting with solicitors all takes time. And this is time away, in Ralph's case, from patients that he needed to be caring for.

Over the ensuing years, Ralph joined other practices and business partners with good working and property agreements and there were a number of times when people moved, agreements were dissolved and new ones started. There were no difficulties with these. Effective agreements can really smooth the passage of change.

A great coping skill is to have and be able to call on a variety of personal and work-based networks of support when the going gets tough. In Ralph's case having good working agreements to underpin the vital relationships turned out to be helpful.

> Who would you turn to for support in a crisis? Which of your professional colleagues, and indeed competitors, would you turn to for advice?

Focusing your passion

In coping with this calamity and with the help of Jackie, Ralph had to maintain his dental practice whilst also searching for new premises and negotiating with Town Planners for change of use to a dental practice. All this was happening in the context of being let down by contracts and a family member.

This experience led Ralph to spend nearly 20 years taking an active role in the British Dental Association, starting locally and ending up filling strategic roles within the regional and national dental community in England.

> If you were in a position where a standard contract let you down, would this motivate you to ensure others don't experience the same problems as yourself?

Conclusion

Calamities can have consequences that linger long after the event. In Ralph's case, it took one to two years to organise and move his dental practice to another part of town. The family issues continued for many years.

Annotated bibliography and references

An Internet search will elicit many sites suggesting they can provide you with advice on your specific issues. As with any unknown source you should take these at face value and do your own homework before committing yourself to spending any money or accepting their advice.

If you would like to learn more about the **UK Landlord & Tenant Acts** then see http://www.landlordzone.co.uk/acts.htm. In other countries, the legalities may differ significantly.

A good source of information and support comes from your professional body, if you are a member. Most **professional groups** offer some level of legal advice as part of the annual subscription.

A UK Government site http://www.sbs.gov.uk/ champions smaller businesses. It is full of useful resources and links.

Chapter 6

"Charities; cash counts"

"People who soar are those who refuse to sit back, sigh and wish things would change. They neither complain of their lot nor passively dream of some distant ship coming in. Rather, they visualise in their minds that they are not quitters; they will not allow life's circumstances to push them down and hold them under."

Charles R. Swindoll

Introduction

In this chapter a Rotarian shares his experiences in turning round a large national charity and supporting it through a period of financial recovery.

Key themes

Charities are businesses too

Most businesses are run by people who have a passion and enthusiasm for their work; they are driven by their personal values – and, most importantly, they balance these heartfelt desires with the more rational 'head' activities such as good management practice.

By their very nature, charities are staffed and run by a complex group of individuals who come from a variety of backgrounds such as local politicians, business people, trade unions and voluntary workers. On the one hand this breadth of community representation is useful; on the other it can stifle and frustrate the need and experience for the application of good business principles.

In this chapter we'll explore the tension of the altruistic approach to managing charities, and how it may impact long term viability.

Knowing when to go

Not only do individuals have different leadership styles, but also different types of leadership are required at different stages of the business. In this particular case, the Rotarian describes how, having completed his work of turning round the finances and operation of the charity, he recognised that he needed to step aside and let someone with a different set of skills and experience move in and develop the business.

Personal experience

"My presentation was greeted with stunned silence. Everyone attending this Emergency Executive Committee Meeting stared at the flip chart which showed that, at the current rate of cash burn, the charity would go bust in eleven months' time. The logic was simple and the data had been there all the time, it was just that no-one had shown them what the implications were in such a blunt way.

Profit, or more usually called surplus when referring to charities, is the difference between total income and total expenses.

Cash flow is the movement of cash in and out of a business.

Positive cash flow arises when the cash received for sales, payments by debtors, reduction in stock etc exceeds the payments for goods and services and expended on fixed assets of the business.

Negative cash flow arises when the cash received for sales, payments by debtors, reduction in stock etc is exceeded by the payments for goods and services and expended on fixed assets in the business.

I had the advantage of coming in as an outsider, new to the executive. I had been invited, a few months earlier, to join the group. I was very busy at work though I had a buyer for my business and that would have freed up my time if the sale went through. So I joined one of the executive meetings and had a close look at all the papers. Four months later my business was indeed sold off and as I was then able to dedicate more time, I joined the Executive Committee of this national charity.

I immediately undertook an appraisal of the state of the finances because, despite the profits looking good over the previous two years, in the order of £150,000–£250,000 per annum, and the balance sheet having a total of £660,000 of cash and realisable assets, I was concerned about the cash burn. Upon further analysis of the figures my suspicions were soon proved right. The Charity was burning cash at the rate of £50,000 to £60,000 per month. Actual income had slumped and budgeted income was too optimistic and yet expenses were increasing, leaving the charity with the prospect of bankruptcy within eleven months due to running out of cash. Income was reducing due to reduced contributions and the loss of a government grant, while expenses were continuing to increase, most specifically overseas travel.

Once the members at the Emergency Meeting had caught their breath, I suggested that we set up a Management Executive

Committee comprising only myself as chairman, the charity chairman and vice chairman. I was given carte blanche to do whatever was necessary for the financial recovery of the organisation, and the chairman and vice chairman acted as checks and balances in case they thought I was going too far. My strategy was to slow the haemorrhaging of cash as quickly as possible, and then to bring the expenses and income in line with each other. The chairman and vice chairman of the charity were supportive of all the actions I took which included parting company with the Chief Executive, the Fund Raising Director and two Departmental Heads, and a reduction in the overseas travel arrangements which saved £200,000.

From the time of my joining the organisation to implementing the recovery plan took only eleven months. Then I resigned. In order for me to accomplish what needed to be done, I'd had to be very tough – very fast. When I walked through the doorway everyone wondered if they were the next to go – this was not good for morale. I was therefore not the right person to continue on the Executive and the organisation needed someone who would give them confidence in the future.

The organisation is still going – indeed, it has gone from strength to strength."

Charities are businesses too

Most charitable work is the business of committees. And the greatest danger with committees is that individuals on the committee get tied up with their own agenda. There is nothing inherently wrong with this; after all, the individuals are volunteering their time and have a very personal reason for doing what is often difficult and time-consuming work. Everyone on the committee wants to do a good job and attends for the right reasons; however, the processes seldom represent good management practice.

The problem comes when large committees, such as the one in this national charity that had twenty-one people at each meeting, have to make decisions. The differing level of interest, as well as experience, lead to conflicting opinions either expressed or unexpressed. Many times decisions are simply not made at meetings, and as was the case for this charity, the meetings were too infrequent (quarterly) for any real tracking of business performance to take place.

When the Rotarian presented the finding of his analysis of the accounts he was confronted with comments such as *"we're not a business you know"*, *"that doesn't apply to us"*, and *"our rules are different"*. However, the management basics are the same.

Charitable organisations are focused on aiding third parties, often disadvantaged ones. Thus any discussion about reducing budgets or stopping services becomes a difficult one for the management team and will bring to the fore any personal interests of those involved in running the organisation.

The same applies to discussion about profit. To some individuals, the concepts of profit and charity do not align. They feel to some extent this may make running a charity far more difficult than running a commercial operation.

> On which committees do you serve? Are you comfortable with the balance between discussion and action?
>
> What motivates you to work on the committee? In what way do you ensure this doesn't get in the way of the business of the organisation?
>
> How business like are the processes? How do you know they are business like?
>
> Do you understand all the paperwork that is sent to you and if you have a specific committee role, such as Treasurer, are you aware of your obligations?

Knowing when to go

At the beginning this Rotarian spent a full six weeks, seven days a week, working on the issues. Thereafter it consumed around one day per week of his time. This is a fairly intense commitment and individuals who work on crises often find it difficult to let go.

A leader who steps in to help resolve a calamity needs to demonstrate a high level of self-awareness. In this story, the Rotarian knew when to step out of the limelight and let someone else, with a different approach, take over and continue to lead the organisation.

How do you spot when someone isn't self-aware?

- They repeat the same mistakes, almost unknowingly
- When they can't explain their own logic
- They appear unable to convert subjectivity into objectivity
- By constantly reacting on instinct which produces poor results
- When there are discrepancies between how they view themselves and how others do

In this case the Rotarian was sufficiently self-aware to know that his productive time had come to an end with this organisation and that he needed to move on.

How do you help someone who lacks this self-awareness to discover what they need to do? By feedback. Neutral and non-judgmental statements of what you have observed and the effect of what you have observed is one way to help others gently develop an

"Sit loosely in the saddle of life."

Robert Louis Stevenson

increased awareness of themselves. This takes time and needs to be managed carefully.

In this book, almost every leader who survived and coped with their calamity demonstrated a good deal of self-awareness.

> Have you ever left a job or given up a task because you knew you were no longer the right person for the work? If so, what were the specific reasons?
>
> Have you every continued in a role when, in hindsight, you wished you had left earlier? With hindsight, what do you know now that would have helped you make the decision to leave earlier?

Conclusion

The happy conclusion for this charity was to become cash flow positive and then to generate enough profit to spend on good works.

There was an added bonus – a significant one. The Rotarian, in his President's year chose this national charity as his Club's specific focus of the year. At the end of the year, a cheque for £250,000 was handed over to the charity. **Yes, £250,000!**

For services to Rotary, this Rotarian was awarded the Paul Harris Fellowship medal for this work.

Annotated bibliography and references

Charitable work and fund raising is a tough business. *Sweet Charity; The Role and Workings of Voluntary Organisations* by Chris Hanvey and Terry Philpot will provide you with some history and context for these types of organisations in the UK, as well as some practical guidance for trustees operating a charity.

Every country will have its own rules and regulations for charities. The Charities Commission is the regulator and registrar for charities in England and Wales. Its website http://www.charity-commission.gov.uk/ contains all the information needed as well as advice on how to manage the accounts for charities.

Paul Harris Fellowship Award

This is the highest award granted by Rotary and was set up to commemorate the work of Paul Harris who founded Rotary in 1905.

In the UK the award is made to people for service in the ideals of Rotary. The people to whom the award is given do not have to be Rotarians.

Chapter 7

"Overblown"

"Do you have the patience to wait until the mud settles and the water is clear? Can you remain unmoving till the right action arises by itself."
Tao Te Ching

Introduction

Some calamities are subtle. They creep up on you, leaving you facing adversity when you weren't really expecting it. Then you deal with them, and they creep away, just like they arrived.

In this chapter, pharmacist John Vooght shares his story about how a sideline nearly destroyed his business because it grew too large. In fact, there were times when he wasn't sure which was the key business.

Key themes

Sticking to the knitting

Basic business principles suggest that knowing your niche and working within it, is good for business. But what do you do when a new and profitable niche presents itself? And if this niche is allied, but not so entirely linked to the core business?

The story in this chapter covers a period of around twenty years where a High Street pharmacy took on the niche of selling wheelchairs, and the ensuing success that endangered the regular business.

Letting go

Many adverse events need immediate action to set the resolution ball rolling. In this example, the action was a more understated series of events that gently put the pharmacy back on course.

One of the key factors in this approach was the ability of John to let go of what had become a fun, lucrative and interesting part of his business, and as it became more specialised, refer his customers on to other more appropriate dealers.

Competition is good

Business and marketing plans bristle with statements about the market, demand, supply and the competition. A predominant tactic is to find ways to outwit the competition and to take their business to increase your own profitability. However, sometimes, your competitor might just be the person or organisation who solves the problem for you.

Personal experience

From his roots on the Wirral, John Vooght went to the Sunderland School of Pharmacy where he obtained B.Pharm (London) and M.Phil degrees. He then worked in industry in Kings Langley before moving to community pharmacy in Aylesbury in 1971.

"In hindsight, I think the point at which the whole situation got out of hand was when we had to rent a warehouse to store our stock of wheelchairs. It was a big step and meant we had to take on extra staff just for this part of the business.

We'd managed for 5 years, but then the wheelchairs started to get more sophisticated and we had to hold a greater range in stock a well as more parts. Apart from adding the warehouse to our operations it also seemed like we could not keep up with the rate of new products.

So how does a regular High Street pharmacy get into selling wheelchairs? Our business was of the traditional kind, started in 1923, focusing on a wide range of products including perfumes, toiletries and cosmetics. As times moved on we felt the need to do something different and more professional.

Sir Ludwig Guttman started the Stoke Mandeville Spinal Injuries Centre just after the Second World War. His successor, Jack Walsh, was the consultant who spotted the wheelchair in our shop window.

Sir Ludwig felt that being a paraplegic should not be an isolated existence in a wheelchair. He encouraged his patients to be physically active. Many of them were under 30 years of age so he set about building the Stoke Mandeville Sports Stadium, mainly for the use of the disabled. He created the National and International Paraplegic Games.

In the 1960s a sales representative from Everest & Jennings Wheelchairs suggested that a wheelchair could be put in the shop window to see if they would sell. Our pharmacy is in the same town as the world-famous Stoke Mandeville Hospital Spinal Injuries Unit so we had a natural market. The Spinal Unit took patients from all over the world, and one of the doctors at the hospital, on seeing the wheelchair in our window, started asking us to supply his private patients, many of whom were from the Middle East. It was difficult for overseas patients to obtain wheelchairs, so it was agreed that I should stock and supply this equipment. I then went on to supply patients with other necessary surgical items, on and after their discharge from hospital.

In the 1960s and early 1970s wheelchairs, although very basic, would sometimes take at least six to eight weeks to arrive, so by keeping a stock of them we built up strong customer support very quickly.

I joined the pharmacy in 1971 and took over the wheelchair part of the business, along with carrying out my regular pharmacist duties. Wheelchair sales boomed for nearly ten years, helped enormously by the Paraplegic Games that were held locally every 4 years.

Then in the early 1980s someone else started a business in town, selling only wheelchairs. And this time he was focusing on more expensive and sophisticated versions. Customers were demanding the more technologically advanced versions from me, including mechanised options and I was having difficulty satisfying their needs. There were different colours, different upholstery, different size wheels and the like. And I was a pharmacist who had other duties in the business and the wheelchair focus was taking me away from the core of what we were supposed to be doing.

As an interim step I tried to stave off any major change by hiring someone else to take over this part of the business, but that didn't work out. So in the end, I decided to stick with the pharmacy and rather than take any drastic action, I chose to refer customers who wanted the new wheelchairs to the new guy in town.

Wheelchair sales gradually declined. I let sales find their own level over the 7 years they took to fall off to the point at which they are now negligible. In hindsight I feel I made the right decision in just letting the business drop off slowly as this was less hassle for me, and certainly I didn't want to upset my customers who would come to me for other reasons as well.

The last couple of years selling wheelchairs had become very frustrating and stressful for me as it became so difficult to meet the demands of the customers. In the end I was relieved when the business fell off. It was also helpful to have a competitor in town who could take over the business. I learnt that sometimes it's good to refer your own customer on to someone else, especially when it is the right thing for the customer.

Looking back it is difficult to see how I could have drawn up a formal business plan at each stage of the journey. Instead, we used our business sense at the time and when necessary, had a long hard think about what we were trying to achieve. At one stage the wheelchair business grew so large that it might have killed the core business, but as we use a weed killer, we got it under control, and our High Street pharmacy continues today – though I have retired."

> "Some people will never learn anything, because they understand too soon."
>
> Alexander Pope

Recall a time when you felt your business, or a part of it, was out of control.

Do you think this was because something had grown too large?

What was that and how could you have dealt with it?

Sticking to the knitting

The job of the sales representative is to engage your interest and get you to buy something; maybe even something you didn't want or need. When the wheelchair was put in the window of the pharmacy, no-one knew what would happen. There were no business plans agreed. It was only a one off thought by the sales representative who was looking to increase his sales. For better or worse it set off a train of activity that went on for at least twenty years.

When a niche market like this develops it can be very seductive. The financial rewards can be great and it is tempting to use these types of activities to prop up a business that has a weak core business. In the case of John and his pharmacy, the core business was good, it was only that the wheelchair business eventually got out of proportion and unmanageable without shifting the core business to selling wheelchairs and having the pharmacy as second string.

There are no right or wrong ways to handle the niche that outgrows you. Some steps that may help avoid a situation become a dire calamity, such as the collapse of the core business are:

1. **Be aware**; when is a niche a niche? Spot when something that is not part of your core business appears to be taking off
2. **Set your sights**; what are the limits within which you expect this niche to perform?
3. **Review frequently**; keep the niche under your control, regardless of the rewards
4. **Take action**; when your core business is threatened
5. **Change strategy**; if appropriate, consider whether it is time for the niche business to become the core business

What is the core business in your organisation?

Do you have any growing niche areas that could get out of control?

Letting go

In telling his story, John shared how he learned to let go of a piece of the business that had been his for many years. And to let go in a piece by piece fashion, nothing dramatic, just a subtle change of direction.

You might think that this was not an actual calamity and that disaster was averted. However, the calamity, the adverse situation was that the pharmacy business was impacted and so was John, who was being torn in different directions. For some people, their calamities are of horror, immediacy and crisis, for others, it is the accumulation of years of small and seemingly at the time, inconsequential actions.

Changing course is a tricky time for any business dependent on loyal customers. One of the risks John faced was creating a problem by announcing they would no longer sell or repair wheelchairs; that may have lost them many customers. By gently referring those customers they could no longer serve due to their new demands, to another business in town, he maintained a good relationship with them.

John himself had to let go of what had, at times, been a fun and important part of his life. His involvement in the Paraplegic Games, which had become a large part of his life – 20 years – came to an end.

This story is a good example of how organisations, the individuals within them, and their environments, all adapt and evolve over time, with little planning or guidance. It all started with a small event, the sales representative putting a wheelchair in the window, and then numerous unplanned events happened, which could not be predicted or managed in detail. All those involved participated in ways that made sense for them; it is history and hindsight that allows us to make overall sense of what happened.

Look back over the last ten to twenty years.

How much planning did you do to get to where you are now?

How much of it just 'sort of' evolved?

What are the implications of this for your future?

What actions might you take now?

Competition is good

Ever noticed how the car dealerships all congregate in one part of town? Although they are in competition with each other, they have the benefit that a customer attracted to one business, say by advertising, may then also come along and visit theirs.

John's case with competition was a little different. At first, when a competitor set up to provide a better quality and more expensive wheelchair he felt threatened. Though he realised that for a while they had a different customer base so there would be no problem. In the end, when John's customers demanded a sophistication that he preferred not to deliver, referring them on to competitor ended up a positive step.

If the pharmacy had decided to compete with their new competitor they may have ended up in a worse calamity. Instead, John learnt to work with and alongside the new business in a form of collaboration that suited both their needs.

Conclusion

When John reflected on this story one overriding feeling was that of having had some fun, particularly being involved in the wheelchair games – and then how hard it was to move on when what had become such a large part of his life, not just working life, was, itself, moving on.

A key theme in this chapter is the ability of a leader to feel the ebb and flow of their business, their market and their opportunities. John chose not to rush or push plans through. Instead, he let market forces take their course and adjusted and trimmed his operation accordingly. This is not unlike a riverboat captain who needs only a light touch on his steering as he senses the flow of his environment.

Annotated bibliography and references

Many business books are written with corporations in mind. *Successful Marketing for the Small Business; A Practical Guide* by Dave Patten, 2001, is a very practical and down-to-earth book focusing all marketing issues that small businesses need to know about.

The story in this chapter is a good example of a **complex adaptive system** at work. If you are interested in the theory of self-organising systems, then there are very many books available, covering all aspects and levels. An Internet search, using the phrase "complex adaptive systems" or a visit to any good bookstore will provide you with a good selection.

Chapter 8

"A "locky" business"

"True life is lived when tiny changes occur."

Leo Tolstoy

Introduction

There is an old adage that says that no snowflake likes to be responsible for the avalanche! The lesson behind this is the potential impact that seemingly small actions and incidents can have.

In this chapter, Mr X describes a small incident in a prison, which in itself was a mishap, and if not dealt with appropriately, could have been much worse. Why "Mr X"? Well, he is subject to the Official Secrets Acts so he needs to remain unidentified.

Key themes

Count the fleas and not the elephants

Large organisations for which safety is a prime concern, such as nuclear plants and the aviation industry, know that attention to detail is paramount. One bolt left on the deck of an aircraft carrier can be enough to bring down an aircraft if it gets sucked into an engine. Or one chisel unaccounted for in a prison could be used to injure someone very badly – as was the case for Mr X.

Policies, procedures, processes and practices can help reduce the probability of system failure. However, concentrating on these at a high level in the organisation without seeing how they work at their most fundamental operating level can render them useless.

Vigilance

Closely linked with the theme above, this is made distinct in this chapter as it was such a vital point in Mr X preventing the situation escalating into a major calamity.

Quick and focused action

Throughout this book there are examples that range on a continuum from "Fast reaction" to "Slow reaction". The speed at which action needs to take place is very much determined by the context. So in the previous chapter, John Vooght's reaction was appropriately fairly slow. In comparison, Mr X had to act extremely fast, taking responsibility and ensuring the situation was resolved speedily.

Personal experience

Mr X is unable to provide any background information on himself as this story is subject to the Official Secrets Act.

"The moment I pulled at the padlock and it came away in my hand my heart sank and then my pulse raced. It was the last day of the winter term in the Prison where I taught young prisoners and my wife and daughter were waiting for me in the car outside. We were going out for lunch and I was in a rush but knew I needed to check that all the rooms and cupboards were locked before I left.

The wood working room had benches with cupboards underneath where all the tools were stored. At a quick glance they appeared locked. I decided to actually pull each padlock, just to make sure. The fifth cupboard lock was the one that dropped open. I checked the tools inside and they all seemed to be there. Then I noticed a large chisel was missing.

I immediately left the room and rang security to advise them that there was a large chisel on the loose in the prison. When they arrived we searched the woodwork room again just to make sure it hadn't been misplaced. All other classrooms were checked – nothing.

To get out of the Educational block there were some steps into a well where the inmates would be checked before returning to their wing. In that well some repair work was underway to repair damage to the polystyrene panels in the ceiling. A security mirror was used to check behind the tiles in the ceiling and a chisel was found in there. It was obviously put there by an inmate in anticipation of doing something with it.

There was a great sigh of relief when it was found as everyone knew that would also mean one less problem that might occur over the Christmas period. It also meant we had avoided a full search of the entire prison which would have meant a significant amount of disruption and inconvenience to both the staff and the inmates.

I eventually made it to lunch where I reflected over the incident. It was such an awful feeling when I found the chisel was missing. I went quite cold as I realised the significance of what it meant. I certainly don't want to repeat that again and it has taught me the importance of being vigilant. Although I could easily have rushed out to meet my family, the extra couple of minutes I spent were vital. It also reminded me just how easily it is to be surprised when we least expect it.

This wasn't the fault of any specific person. Working in the environment we do, it is important that everyone understands the need to pay attention to detail, to be observant and that we can't afford to relax – at any time."

> "The longer we dwell on our misfortunes, the greater is their power to harm us."
>
> Voltaire

Count the fleas and not the elephants

Our language is filled with imagery to explain how big events are triggered by small, almost inconsequential acts – "The straw that broke the camel's back" – is one such example. This is not an unfamiliar concept when we consider our lives in general; it is, however, one that is not often considered in our work lives.

How may times have we tried to make something happen by complicated and detailed back room planning to discover later that implementing the changes seems so difficult. Yet something minor happens and a whole set of changes take place. In the first case we are trying to control the change – usually to no avail, and in the second case, we often feel at the whim of some outside force. This "outside force" is usually nothing more than our inability to sense what is happening in our environment. Changes happen all the time and many of these are out of sight of our direct focus of business, or of our personal attention.

Mr X's story shows how minute the attention to detail needs to be in some circumstances. If he trusted his eyesight he would have left the chisel at large in the prison. Instead he used a second sense, and touched the locks, double-checking himself.

From the perspective of the prison staff they would have had no knowledge of the missing chisel until it was put to use – undoubtedly not a good use. The chisel would have been their "snowflake", their "straw" that ended up creating a bigger crisis.

We have good intentions to be focused and pay attention to detail, but our view gets blocked, usually by what we perceive to be bigger or more pressing issues. We start to see elephants. Our view gets blocked.

Reflect on a recent mishap. With the benefit of hindsight, can you identify the "straw that broke the camel's back?"

What "elephants" can you identify that blocked your view so you didn't see the issue coming?

How can you avoid this happening in the future?

Vigilance

The Oxford Dictionary defines *vigilance* as

- Watchfulness
- Caution
- Circumspection

Mr X displayed all of these characteristics in his role at the prison. His environment demanded that he take extra care in his duties. However, is vigilance a leadership quality unique to only security and safety-focused sectors? Unlikely.

These characteristics are useful for any person who is responsible for staff members. Watching over their safety and work conditions, their stress levels, their ability to carry out their roles; being cautious about your own interactions with others so you get the best out of them; and not always rushing in – or out – of situations without first thinking about the circumstances or issues at hand.

Vigilance means being attentive to circumstances outside yourself. We can easily become preoccupied with our own thoughts and ambitions. Mr X could easily have been distracted by the fact his wife and daughter were waiting outside for him in their car, a pleasant lunch ahead of him. Instead he kept focused on the task in hand.

What do you think requires your vigilance?

Is it something at home or work?

Why is this necessary?

Does vigilance come naturally or are you someone more easily distracted?

What are the implications of this for you?

Quick and focused action

How quickly do you move in a crisis? Mr X took a decision and made a phone call in minutes. Then the prison staff immediately started searching for the chisel. Every minute mattered. Not all crises need this speed of action.

When to move quickly

- You have a good idea about what the correct course of action should be

- That if you don't act, then the knock on impact, to you or someone else, will be worse
- You believe that the crisis you are facing could escalate very quickly

> When was the last time you took really quick action to avoid a situation getting worse? Was your timing right?
>
> With hindsight, what would you do differently now?

Conclusion

It never crossed Mr X's mind not to report the missing chisel and to go to lunch – he would be insulted to think this was even an option for consideration! Yet how often do we consciously make the decision to let "something slip" because it appears "small and of little consequence". A clear lesson from this chapter is the importance of considering the consequences of our actions – or inactions.

Mr X didn't hesitate to report the problem, although he or another member of staff might have to go through a variety of processes to review what had happened. He knew that implications of a chisel on the loose were far bigger than an internal review. He also did so in the knowledge that the review would be a constructive one and nothing that apportioned blame in any accusing way. This is a characteristic of a learning organisation and one that many organisations have difficulty getting to grips with.

The first chapter in this book, about the needle stick injury in hospital, is one where the doctor was worried about what would happen if the incident was reported. The environment he works in is not as conducive to learning from experience as that of Mr X.

Annotated bibliography and references

The best book on Highly Reliable Organisations (HRO) is by Karl Weick and Kathleen Sutcliffe, *Managing the unexpected; Assuring high performance in the age of complexity*, University of Michigan Business School Management Series.

If you are interested in exploring more detail about the science that lies behind the "straw that broke the camel's back" then an Internet search using the phrase "sensitivity to initial conditions" will provide you with an extensive range of reading.

Curious about Mr X and the Official Secrets Act? Check out http://www.hmso.gov.uk/acts/acts1989/Ukpga_19890006_en_1.htm for more details.

Chapter 9

"Gaining from losing"

"He who knows others is wise. He who knows himself is enlightened."
Loa-tzu

Introduction

At the core of every calamity is an individual. Some events are precipitated by world wars, others by factory errors or companies going out of business. It would be easy to analyse disasters by looking at the systems, by agreeing causes and factors, reasons and motives. However, the real learning comes from looking in depth at what happened to the individuals involved.

In this chapter Roger Simmons shares his personal transformation along the road to recovering from being made redundant.

Key themes

Downshifting

The modern day trap is a familiar one; work long hours, spend more time commuting, earn enough money to pay for needs and expectations, not enough time at home, more stress etc. Sitting in the traffic jam it's easy to conjure up images of a quieter and more restful life. Sometimes we need a calamity to force us into thinking through our options and choosing the one to shift down to a slightly slower pace of life, that in the most cases is a more enriched one that may make us feel more content.

Defeating ageism

"You lack the experience" or "You don't have the qualifications" feel like reasonable excuses for not getting a job. "You're too old" doesn't, especially when you are 18 years off the normal retirement age.

Companies have traditionally gone for the raw recruits they can mould into their own ways and shunned what can be useful experience. Some companies are, however, realising that older recruits, even those over retirement age, can be good for business. This is especially so in the service sector. Nonetheless, these examples are few. Instead, those who are made redundant, and that is a more common feature nowadays, need to add the battle against ageism to their list of things to do to cope with their calamity.

Personal experience

Roger Simmons started at C&A when only a teenager. After completing his management training he was appointed to run a store at East Ham in London. After three years, in 1983, he moved and opened a new store in Chelmsford. He had three further appointments before his final position in Manchester in 1998.

He is married to Iona and has two children.

"The Director read out a statement that said my job as Store Manager responsible for 100 staff was no longer required and as I had been at the company for a long time I would be paid a generous settlement. I also receive three months pay in lieu of notice.

I was taken through the statement again by someone from Human Resources and then I met the Outplacement Agency. Not that I took in much at the time. I was not allowed back to the office and my personal stuff was sent home. I never got a chance to say goodbye to my colleagues.

In January 1999, at the age of 48 and with fairly substantial family commitments, I found myself out of work. The real tragedy however, was that I had gifted my working life to a large family-owned retailer, C&A. I started there as a Saturday boy aged 16 and moved through the ranks. I had no qualifications outside courses run internally by the company. I had been closeted in a secure and happy working environment for 32 years. This had been at a cost as I had on occasion had to move away from my family so I could continue my career within the company. At the time of my redundancy I was working 300 miles away from my family, seeing them only at the weekend. Retirement was planned for age 56 when I would have had 40 years working time under my belt. It was not to be.

My initial response on receiving the news was shock. I was too numb to consider the consequences. I didn't feel any resentment for what had happened as it had been a good company (and has since closed its UK operations).

C&A was founded by two brothers called Clement and August Brenninkmeyer in Sneek, Holland in 1841. They expanded into the majority of European countries with now approximately 560 stores. They entered the UK market in 1922 with their first store situated in Oxford Street, London, and expanded to over 100 stores when they experienced a dramatic change in fortune. The competition from Matalan and other low cost retailers severely affected their profitability in the mid-1990s as did the decision to introduce central buying for the whole of the European market, thus disbanding national identities. These two factors were the main reasons for the complete closure of all C&A stores in the UK in 2001.

The financial implications were of course very important. Though it soon dawned on me that the real calamity facing me was that I had spent so much time cocooned in one company that I was barely employable by similar retailing companies. Also, my lack of any recognisable qualification was a hindrance. In hindsight I was effectively married to the company and brainwashed into its culture. I'd moved around so much that I had no roots and few friends. The friends I did have were at work and I found it very difficult that I had not been able to say a proper goodbye to them. It was as though the process of being made redundant was something to be ashamed of and to be hidden.

The first decision we made as a family was that we would not move house again. The children were at a crucial stage in their education and my wife, Iona, and I decided that it was important to have some stability in our lives.

I worked with the outplacement agency, attending their offices two to three times a week. A CV was an entirely new concept to me as I had never needed to produce one! The consultant who was allocated to my case was very helpful and supportive. He was a particularly good listener. I kept going there because it was like maintaining a work routine. I think this confused my family as they didn't know what I was doing and I wasn't taking the time, I should have, to be talking with my wife. My self-esteem had taken a knock and I was just doing my best to keep going.

My initial aim was to stay in retailing, however, I found my lack of breadth of experience was limiting. I was also faced with ageist prejudices – 48 years old often being seen as too old to employ. It soon dawned on me that I would have to change my ideas of what constituted a job and career. My empathy was with retailers and I had been working with shopping centre managers so I thought that might be an option. When I visited a colleague to see what he did as a shopping centre manager I was surprised by the amount of control he had. This was a job I wanted.

Guided by the outplacement centre I bought the relevant professional magazines and, by coincidence, the job of centre manager in a town about 15 miles away from home was advertised. I got the job but there was a problem. The salary on offer was almost half what I had been getting and the management company didn't believe that I wasn't just going to use the job as a stepping stone to some other job. It took some convincing but I got the job.

Four years on my life has moved on in many ways. The redundancy caused me to take stock of my life – to downshift. This has provided me with a much enhanced work-life balance. I'm proud to have completed a Certificate in Management that proves to myself that I am capable of gaining formal accreditation for my work. I also

In 1998 the UK Government published proposals for a non-statutory Code of Practice on age discrimination in employment.

Launching the report, the employment minister Andrew Smith said: "By 2006 more than 25% of the workforce will be aged 50 or over. Employers and the wider community cannot afford to discriminate unfairly on the grounds of age. This Government is determined to tackle the problem but cannot do so on its own. We have to work in partnership with business, employees and interested groups, as well as the public … Nevertheless, the action proposed, including a non-statutory Code of Practice [on age discrimination], … will provide a comprehensive and coherent plan to tackle the issue. It is a challenging task, the key to which is changing attitudes towards age and how we judge the ability of all to participate and contribute to the continued growth and development of the economy."

http://www.eiro.eurofound.ie/1998/09/feature/uk9809148f.html

"No one can ever make you feel inferior without your consent."

Eleanor Roosevelt

have far more time now for friendships and for putting back time into community efforts through various local organisations."

> Have you ever been made redundant?
>
> If so, what career implications were there for you?
>
> What qualifications and experience do you have now that would stand you in good stead of getting another job if you were made redundant this week?

Downshifting

This is most often defined as a proactive step towards a lifestyle that is less pressured, probably in a different environment and most likely away from urban areas, and generally always means taking a reduction in income.

Reactive or proactive?

In Roger's case, his downshift was a reactive move created by a surprise redundancy. Many others choose a more proactive approach. So you want to downshift? Consider the following questions and be sure to discuss them thoroughly with anyone close to you who may be affected by your decision:

> How could you benefit from doing less or living in a different style to that to which you have become accustomed?
>
> If you removed money as one of the barriers to doing something different; what would you then do? Where would you live? What job would you like best?

Defeating ageism

The issue of ageism became apparent in the late 1980s and early 1990s as organisations went through "rationalisations" and chose to lose their older employees, either through early retirement or compulsory redundancy programmes. The loss of experience and expertise was balanced against the financial benefits to stakeholders at the time. Also, many employers perceived their older generation of employees, may not be able to keep up with the technological advances and many were not offered training.

In a survey – *Breaking the barriers: A survey of managers' attitudes to age and employment,* J Arrowsmith and AE McGoldrick, Institute of Management, London, 1996 – 55% of 1700 people surveyed believed their company discriminated on the basis of age when it comes to recruitment and retention. The figures for training opportunities and promotion are not much different.

Defeating ageism if you are a leader in an employing organisation

- Check what your formal policies state with regards age for recruitment, training, promotion, retirement etc.
- Gather information about what actually happens and compare this to your policies. For example, check some samples of job applications that have been turned down and see whether there are any age related patterns. Ageism is such a social construct that many people may be turning down applicants without being conscious about their actions. Measurement is an excellent way to make this apparent and to make improvements.

This chapter has concentrated on ageism at the older end of the scale. A similar, though less frequent form is found with the younger generation.

> At what age do you think someone is too old to work in your organisation? Why is this? (There may be some very good reasons)
>
> Have you ever been turned down for a job based on your age? Or have you turned down someone based on his or her age?

Commentary by Sarah Fraser

In 1997, I gave up my senior management post in Esso Petroleum UK Ltd and moved to the public sector. At the time I was on a posting to Esso Finland where I was experiencing a new way of working. There they enjoyed a decent end time to the day as few people worked past 5 pm. In the summer everyone took a whole continuous four weeks off to spend time with their families and relaxing. I realised that having experienced the different work-life balance I could not go back to my old job in the UK.

Like Roger, I had to go through a number of phases in working out what I wanted to do. In the end I too took a job that commanded a significant salary decrease. In return I cut down on my commuting to and from work. I also found myself constrained by the internal Esso training that I had received and after ten years with the company I had no formal accreditation of my experience. I embarked on an Open University degree course more to learn the language of the new culture I was working in – health and social care – than to gain the degree.

The irony is my downshift lasted about three years and I now find myself upshifting slightly though as I work for myself I have more control over my time which means I can organise my work patterns to suit myself.

Ageism is not something I have encountered – yet. My hope is that legislation and common sense reign by the time I reach that stage in my life.

Conclusion

This story is one of triumph over tragedy. On reflection it looks like Roger's life is a far happier and secure one now than what he thought he had before he was made redundant.

Now that's something to think about... ·

Annotated bibliography and references

The Internet School Library Medical Centre is an excellent portal for information about ageism, particularly with regards to education and literature. http://falcon.jmu.edu/~ramseyil/ageism.htm

There are a number of books on downshifting. One that tells it as a move to a more simple lifestyle by living with less is *Downshifting: the guide to happier, simpler living* by Polly Ghazi and Judy Jones (Coronet, 1997).

Nicholas Corder has written *Escape the rat race; downshifting to a richer way* (Elliot Right Way books, 2001). A practical book with plenty of hints and tip and how to start by taking small steps.

Chapter 10

"Risky business"

"All of life is the exercise of risk."

William Sloan Coffin

Introduction

As we've seen in other chapters in this book, there is a fine line between operating a business in an appropriate manner and trying to eliminate risks that could have a negative consequence on the business. In the end, life is a risky business and we encounter hazards everyday; some of these we notice and others have become part of the daily routine. For example, your journey to work may take you down a narrow road where you pass oncoming traffic with a head-on impact speed of around 100 mph, yet your wing mirrors pass with inches to spare – and you don't notice the risk. Because you do it every day.

In this chapter, Dr Helen Falcon, shares her views and personal learning about one of her calamities when she was working as a dentist.

Key themes

Listen to feedback

It is easy to miss or dismiss the complaint of a child or from someone who always seems to be complaining. Yet in these nuggets of feedback are the warning signs that something may be going wrong. Attending to them as early as possible could save a minor inconvenience from becoming a major calamity.

Fix the practical stuff

The most basic errors are the most embarrassing ones. Yet these are the ones which are often the most likely to happen. Why? Because we spend time focusing on what appear to be more important issues. In this chapter, Helen gives an example of calamity based on a very basic and well-known safety issue.

Recognise the limitations of controls

It is not possible to control for all possible adverse events. Eventually a business would become so unwieldy that the business would not get done. A key leadership role is to define and set the boundaries for what level of control is required and how these can best be implemented.

Personal experience

Helen Falcon qualified as a dental surgeon in 1977 and has worked in general and community dental practice and dental public health. At the time of this incident she was Deputy Chief Executive of a Community Healthcare Trust and Clinical Director of the Dental Service.

Even I have got so used to the fact that all children complain when they're at the dentist that I could understand it when a colleague ignored the child who was complaining of a bad taste in his mouth. Until they noticed a strange smell and realised something definitely was wrong.

The dental nurse checked the equipment and quickly discovered that there was something amiss with the water. The tank that fed the three in one syringe that squirts into the mouth of the patients had accidentally been filled with x-ray developing fluid instead of water.

I was shocked when I was told about the incident – shocked that such a basic mistake could be made. However, when I checked the cupboard it was easy to see how. Both the water and the x-ray fluid were in almost identical 5-gallon plastic whitish opaque drums. And both were a clear fluid.

This was a serious matter and I went through the regular reporting procedure for incidents like this. As the senior dentist in the organisation it was very embarrassing to admit to such a basic error both at the time and later at a Board Meeting and I took full responsibility.

The national poisons unit recommended we contact all the patients we'd seen that morning to check there weren't any adverse effects that they were feeling. Fortunately no-one else seemed to have a problem. Everyone we called was pleased we had told them the full story. They thanked us for being open and honest; and no one called their lawyer.

The obvious thing we rectified was the design of the cupboard and we made sure that similar types of containers with dissimilar products were stored well away from each other to avoid confusion.

However, for me the real issue was coming to terms with the limits on what we could do to reduce risk. This incident motivated my team to look at our basic procedures and the design and layout of our workplace. However, it was clear that we couldn't write a procedure for every possible thing that could go wrong. There will always be pressures of work that make us forget something, stress and other human error. Part of resolving this issue was to look at how we worked together, how individuals performed their roles and responded to situations in different ways. As human beings we are very complex – so learning how we operate and work together is an ongoing learning activity.

Listen to feedback

Listening is more than only hearing sounds. It is about being aware of what is going on around you and being able to absorb and make meaning from the information you take in. When we are in a familiar environment it becomes difficult to maintain this awareness as the regular sounds become part of our subconscious; we notice only that which is remarkably different.

Feedback is one of the basic building blocks of communication and learning. Without it, we would not survive for long. The incident described in this chapter went though many stages of feedback; through a reporting system, with patients, with staff and Helen's own personal reflections. By listening and taking the time to work through these processes, lessons can be learnt that can become part of the memory and learning of all those involved.

> "I think self awareness is probably the most important thing towards being champion"
>
> Billie Jean King

We were all reminded that feedback is a two way process and that it is important to be grateful for feedback, to learn and then move, and specifically, not to shoot the messenger.

For Helen it was hard to take responsibility for the actions of an employee, however, that accountability was essential for the incident to be properly resolved. Even more important was the fact the other dentist reported the incident; without which more errors may have occurred in the future. As difficult as it was at the time to deal with the mess, it was an important piece of learning for everyone involved.

> Next time you are in a familiar working environment, take 3 minutes to step back and focus your awareness. What are you taking for granted? Look at it carefully? What do you see or hear?

What happens to our listening skills?

There are three components of active listening (Weaver & Farrell):

(a) **Sensing**; using all our senses to take in information

(b) **Interpreting**; evaluating the meaning of the information

(c) **Checking**; reflecting on what you have heard in an effort to gain a mutual understanding of the speaker's intended message

A lack of awareness to signals coming at us, or a subconscious filtering, can inhibit even the start of a listening process. Even if we do hear what is said, we may interpret it differently from what is meant by the speaker.

For anyone whose role depends on an interaction with someone else (which is probably all of us in the world except for a few hermits), then ability to pay attention and listen is a key factor in both avoiding and coping with calamities.

Fix the practical stuff

Everyone agrees that putting similar containers side by side, with one containing water and the other a colourless but hazardous fluid, is not a good idea. But it happened.

The design and layout of workspace is important, and not only for critical places like dentist surgeries. Offices also need to be laid out well to minimise the risks posed by accidental injury.

Most organisations have safety policies, however, these are often difficult to translate into action in the day-to-day running of the business. In both small and large organisations where safety is paramount and risks are minimised, policies are built into the system through discussion, agenda items, regular audits, reporting schemes etc.

> Take a close look at your workspace. How many potential hazards can you identify within three minutes?

Recognise the limitations of controls

If every process and procedure in the dental surgery was itemised and then worked through step-by-step, very little work would get done. Real safety is achieved when the individuals who work in the organisation raise their awareness and take responsibility for the safety of those they are working with as well as the clients. It is an individual responsibility and one that relies on a great degree of communication and trust.

When last did you walk past a fire door that was propped open by a fire extinguisher?

Can you be sure that your staff always read the labels on containers?

What unsafe practices are you aware of that you feel you should now raise with others and resolve?

Conclusion

We cannot take account of all possible risks. We can, however, design workspace and put in place systems of procedures that minimise the potential for harm. Ultimately we live our lives interacting with other people, and much of our personal safety relies on their actions and on developing trusting relationships so that they will tell us when things go wrong

To err is human – to forgive is divine.

Annotated bibliography and references

Chapter 1 of this book covered resources for medical safety and the human factors element of reducing risk in the workplace.

Important agencies that offer resources to help healthcare practitioners improve safety are the **National Patient Safety Agency** in the UK: www.npsa.nhs.uk. The Institute for Healthcare Improvement Resources site contains links covering these and other relevant topics: http://www.ihi.org/resources/weblinks/

The ability to give and receive feedback is an essential competency for daily living. An excellent book is *The ABCs of Feedback; a Guide for Caring Professionals* by Irwin Rubin & Thomas Campbell (Jossey-Bass, 2003) has a simple behavioural model that can be used in any feedback situation. The model is supplemented by an online tool available from www.temenosinc.com

Managers as facilitators; A practical guide to getting work done in a changing workplace by Richard Weaver & John Farrell; Berrett-Koehler 1997 is an excellent guide and includes a section on active listening.

Chapter 11

"Spilt milk"

"The real voyage of discovery consists not in seeking new landscapes, but in having new eyes."

Marcel Proust

Introduction

Finding the root cause of a calamity can be tricky. In many cases the consequences come from a number of different sources that all interact with each other to give rise to the unpredictable event that you experience. In other cases, the cause could be a simple one.

Dairies processing our daily milk need to be paragons of quality and cleanliness. In this chapter, Des Brazier, former Managing Director of B&M Dairies tells his story of when things went wrong and their challenges in working out why and how it happened.

Key themes

Experience can better technology

It is difficult to remember a time when our lives were not dominated by some form of technology. We take so much for granted in the way we conduct our businesses that it is easy to forget that not everything can be stored on, managed or solved by computers or other equipment.

Despite sophisticated laboratory equipment, the dairy was unable to get to the root of the problem described in this chapter. Until an experienced milk tanker driver walked in…

Breaking routine increases risk

Things tend to go wrong when our routines are disrupted. With routine comes the comfort of knowing that tasks are happening in an orderly and planned way; even if at times this is as much sub-conscious as conscious.

Occasions such as moving house or taking a holiday can disrupt the regular flow of activities, thus increasing the likelihood of something going wrong.

Think twice

In the heat of fixing this calamity, the dairy created another calamity, though not one they immediately felt the effects of.

Personal experience

Des Brazier followed the family tradition started by his grandfather and spent his whole career in the dairy industry; covering retail, wholesale and manufacturing.

He has served on many regional and national committees in the UK including the National Dairyman's Association, the Milk Processor's Council and the Farm Advisory Council with the Ministry of Agriculture.

Ragwort (*Senecio jacobaea*) is also known by the synonyms: St. James-wort. Ragweed. Stinking Nanny. Staggerwort. Dog Standard. Cankerwort. Stammerwort. Growing 2–3ft tall with pretty yellow flowerheads, it is a highly prized herb and used in many tinctures and remedies. However, it is NOT good for cows! It is one of the most frequent causes of plant stock poisoning of animals. Each plant can produce up to 150,000 seeds with a germination rate of 70%. And these seeds can lay dormant for up to 20 years.

Fat hen (*Chenopodium album*) is considered by many populations in the world as a very palatable and nutritious food. This herb is considered more of an undesirable weed than a poison for cows.

"The stench was dreadful. It was an organic type of smell – very nasty. It certainly was not a smell we would expect to have in our milk processing plant and indeed it was not one we had ever experienced before.

We took a sample and ran it through all the checks possible in our laboratory. Quality measurement was a big part of what we did so we had a decent lab. Milk had to be handled very carefully and there was no margin for error or smells of any kind. And milk is susceptible to taints.

Despite using all known quality tests nothing registered as out of the ordinary. We were stumped.

There was little we could do other than throw away 2000 gallons of milk and go through a rigorous clean up process. Fortunately this was the only time we ever had to throw that much milk away.

A couple of days after the incident, a tanker driver driving one of the milk lorries walked in and sniffed the air. He immediately declared "Ragwort and Fat Hen." We asked him to explain and he said that he could smell the milk of cows that had eaten the Ragwort and Fat Hen weeds. So now we knew what the cause was, we had to do some investigation to find out whose cows were eating these weeds before it happened again.

We tracked the problem back to only 100 gallons of a high fat content milk. The farm owner had gone on holiday and left a cowhand in charge. His job was to set up the electric fence so day by day it shifted across the pasture, enabling the cows to have fresh grazing each day. The only problem was he forgot to do this and the cows became so hungry they ate the weeds which they would normally regard as inedible.

When the owner of the farm returned from holiday she was very upset about what happened. We lost 2000 gallons of milk in the process and the main loss was a financial one.

However, we did make a mistake in the way we got rid of the spoilt milk. Without thinking, it got tipped down the drain which in retrospect was not a good idea. We should have spent more time planning how to deal with the milk and ensuring it didn't get disposed of this way.

The main lesson I learnt was that with all the technology we had invested in and become reliant on, it took an old countryman with real experience to solve the problem for us. I realised the limitation of machines and renewed my appreciation and value for all things human and experiential."

> Recall a time when you couldn't find the cause of what went wrong? You might have felt there should be a simple answer but you couldn't find it. Were you relying on technology?
>
> Was there a dissonance between what the technology was suggesting and what your intuition was proposing? Did this matter?

Experience can better technology

There are apocryphal tales about the rate at which knowledge is expanding and therefore the growing importance of computers and other instruments to handle it. In the hunger for more knowledge and the ability to apply it, many organisations are employing *knowledge management* strategies and techniques.

Simply put, knowledge management is a way in which explicit and tacit knowledge is captured and stored so it can be used later. In the example in this chapter, the tanker driver had some tacit knowledge about the weeds that the cows had eaten. Tacit because he was not aware of this knowledge, he had not gone to school and passed exams specifically about this. He gained it from experience. His knowledge is very difficult to codify and pass on to others. Other dairies may want to be able to tap into this knowledge but it would be very difficult to share, though Des could have written some notes and shared them with owners of other dairies.

This sharing of information, even across competitors, has become standard practice in many industries and is one way of organisations avoiding calamities by learning from others. The more similar to their own organisations, the easier it is to apply the lessons learnt.

> "A problem well-defined is half solved."
>
> John Dewey

> Think of a key member of staff in your organisation.
>
> What knowledge does that person hold that if they left you would miss?
>
> What can you do to capture some of that knowledge?

Breaking routine increases risk

The farmer came back from holiday to discover a calamity of her own. For some reason, a trusted employee slipped up on a very basic procedure and she faced the embarrassment of her cows being the ones to have eaten the weeds.

Moving the electric fences is a very basic procedure for any farm hand, and one that she would not normally have needed to remind him about. However, no doubt with her away he was distracted – and distractions are key times when calamities occur.

> One of the difficulties of a routine is spotting one! Try and recall something that is very routine for you.
>
> What circumstances might upset this routine?
>
> What might you do to prevent the upset whilst enduring the circumstances?

Think twice

Des regretted not thinking more about how his dairy disposed of the milk. One of the themes throughout this book has been the need to take quick action, however, the speed of this action needs to be balanced against the risks involved.

Checking that your solution is not creating another calamity is a very important step; even if that calamity may be felt by someone other than yourself.

Conclusion

For Des and his team this was a memorable event, not just for the overpowering and horrid smell, but for the way that the problem was solved. Despite their quality procedures and laboratories they couldn't solve the problem without the unexpected help of an unlikely person. They were fortunate the tanker driver came into their dairy when he did, else they would never have found the cause of the smell.

Annotated bibliography and references

The Complete Idiot's Guide to Knowledge Management by Melissie
Clemmons Rumizen, Alpha, 2002
> An excellent introductory guide to the concepts and principles behind
> knowledge management, written in an engaging and easy to read
> manner. Highly recommended.

If you're looking for ways to identify and work out what to do with the
weeds (or perhaps they are herbs) in your garden or field then *Weeds:
Friend or Foe; An Illustrated Guide to Identifying, Taming and Using Weeds*
by Sally Roth (Carroll & Brown; 2002).

If you are curious about how milk is processed then see
www.dairynetwork.com which covers a huge range of topics, aimed at the
dairy industry. For a more simple read, the Australian site
http://www.fao.org/ag/aga/agap/lps/dairy/DAP/MPG.htm has some simple
guides.

Chapter 12

"In the public eye"

"If you always do what you always did; you'll always get what you always got."

Unknown

Introduction

It's bad enough coping with an adverse event in private, it's even more challenging to have your every move under the scrutiny of the public eye. And to have the public in your face, mouthing insults and waving petitions will create a very tense and stressful situation.

In this chapter, Roy Collis shares his experience of presenting what appeared to be an objective set of recommendations for his County Library Service to the Council – and by implication – also the public.

Key themes

Be prepared to stand up for your beliefs

When the going gets tough, the tough have to get really good at holding their ground – to misquote a common saying. Roy had spent two years working on a detailed assessment of the County's Library Service and had produced a package of recommendations aimed at providing the best quality public library service that resources would permit. He firmly believed that his recommendations were the best for the community and the taxpayer. Although he faced severe personal pressure to change these he held ground.

Think ahead

Roy's calamity was the response of the public for which he was unprepared. Some scenario planning and preplanning may have reduced the impact of this.

Personal experience

"The situation hit rock bottom when my six-year-old son, along with other children playing on the village green, was asked to write his name on a petition! We had the media visiting our home, my wife was being insulted in the local shop and we were getting phone calls at all times of the day and night.

After leaving Devizes Grammar School in 1961, started work with Wiltshire County Library, before becoming a Qualified Librarian after attending Birmingham Library School in 1964–66. He was appointed County Librarian of Buckinghamshire in January 1983.

Since his early retirement in October 1996, he has chaired a number of national and regional committees in the library field, including the Prison Libraries Group of the Library Association. Following retirement he prepared a new edition of the Association's Guidelines for Prison Libraries, published in December 1997, and was elected an Honorary Fellow of the Library Association in 1999.

He is now a Regional Coordinator for The Royal Star & Garter Home for Disabled Ex-Servicemen and Women; Chairman of the Connexions Board for Milton Keynes, Oxfordshire and Buckinghamshire; Chairman of Bucks Community Action [the Rural Community Council], and involved in a range of voluntary sector groups. He was appointed a Deputy Lieutenant for Buckinghamshire in 2001, and lives in Wing with his wife Pamela.

In 1983, as the Buckinghamshire County Librarian I was tasked with developing a recovery plan for a service dying on its feet. For three years we had not purchased any new books and the infrastructure of maintaining a service of small libraries and mobile services to a predominantly rural community was proving a financial struggle. As the new Chief I recognised that the network of small libraries would not be sustainable given the financial outlook. I was given a mandate to modernise the library service.

I launched a comprehensive appraisal of every branch and mobile library, and compared our provision with national and international standards. This included surveys and investigations into aspects such as the pattern of opening hours, staffing, whether the small rural libraries were in the right places, where to give priority to future projects, where the users came from, their rate of use etc.

I, with the team working on this, came up with a comprehensive package of twenty recommendations of changes all to be delivered within existing resources, namely a far more efficient service. We proposed a better pattern of evening and Saturday opening sessions, and we were to become one of the first County Library services in the country to link all 42 Branch Libraries via an on-line computer system; all 7 mobile libraries had off-line links to this stock control and circulation system. Users could then take items out of any library and return them to any other in the County.

Our research had discovered that the rate of use of the mobile units was higher than the smaller static libraries so this was reflected in a proposal to close eight small village-based services and replace them with one mobile library. And it was this proposal that provoked an extraordinary reaction.

All of this seemed a very rational, objective and logical process, until all hell let loose. It is very important that all meetings in Local Government are held in public where both strategic and operational decision-making can be transparent, and where the public, who have voted in their council members, can take part. This meant that when

I presented the plans in March 1986 there was an instant reaction from the public and the media, most of whom concentrated only on the closures of the eight small libraries. It's not possible to go to consultation until the committee has seen the papers, yet as soon as they have seen the papers, everything is in the public domain!

Community activists sprung up and many local community meetings were held, many of which I attended. These were mostly heated and I took a lot of negative energy on from communities who had collected petitions to keep open their libraries.

For the Council Members this was also quite a problem as the library service was one way they kept close contact with their voters. In the end, when the decision was made as to whether to accept the package or not, it went, by one vote, to keeping the status quo.

I was surprised, and still am, at the level of revolt over the recommendations. But when I think about it, libraries are neutral places, with information and for many communities they are part of the life support system where people of all ages meet and many will also provide the role of local halls.

In the six months between presenting the recommendations and the vote to keep the status quo I had a tremendous amount of pressure that I had to deal with. Much of it felt very personal. I have broad shoulders though at times it was difficult to keep my cool. I focused on sticking to the script and tried to be as objective as possible and not get drawn into any of the rivalries between libraries.

Although it was tough at the time, the white water period was soon over and I buckled down to turning our libraries into the best in the country, which they became. By 1996 we were delivering the highest book issues per head of population of any County Library service in England or Wales, the highest number of non-book issues, the highest income generation and the highest number of visitors. And the work I carried out in the 1980s helped me as the blueprint for the newer modernised services in the late 1990s.

In conclusion it is worth noting that three of the small libraries were eventually closed! This was due to lack of use, and several of the others were extended with financial help from Parish Councils or community groups. This adds weight to the old adage that a prophet is rarely appreciated for his pronouncements!"

> "Sometimes things which at the moment may be perceived as obstacles – and actually be obstacles, difficulties, drawbacks – can in the long run result in some good end which would not have occurred if it had not been for the obstacle."
>
> Steve Allen

Have you ever had to deal with the media?

If so, in what way was it stressful?

If not, how might you imagine it would stress you?

Have you ever presented what you believe to be a rational and objective proposal, to be hit back with an emotive response?

If so, how did you cope?

Be prepared to stand up for your beliefs

Roy found that this incident reinforced his conviction that he would have to be prepared to stand up – in front of angry crowds – and hold his ground. It would have been easy to roll over or to leave the job and let someone else manage the problem.

Instead, he took responsibility and accountability for seeing the crisis through to a conclusion. He knew it would take six to twelve months out of his life while he restored peace in the various communities and he got on with it. He knew that the short-term pain would be repaid later for longer gain.

And handsomely repaid it was as the Library Services, with all the passion from the public, became well used.

Another outcome from Roy's experience was a review of consultation processes. The public reaction to the proposals made all members of the Council aware of how important the library service was.

> "Courage is contagious. When a brave man takes a stand, the spines of others are often stiffened."
>
> Billy Graham

When were your beliefs last tested?

Did you hold your ground or give way? (Sometimes, giving way is just as good as holding your ground, what's important is to know when to do which.)

Think ahead

Roy was unable to control the way the messages were delivered to the public and unable to conduct a consultation process before his recommendations went before any committee. So it was difficult for him to gauge what the reactions might have been. However, he could have benefited from some scenario planning and had a number of plans in place to help manage any untoward reaction.

Public consultations are difficult to manage, and those that are concerned with changes to the social fabric of a community, such as closing libraries, hospitals, building new housing estates etc. are bound to cause consternation and a passionate reaction from many local residents.

What regulations do you have in your organisation for consulting the public on any activities you plan to carry out?

Perhaps you've participated in a local activity where you've been someone trying to keep a facility open in your community. What ideas do you have that would have helped the process for you, that you could provide to, for example, Roy, as advice?

Conclusion

Roy's experience was personally distressing and continued for a number of months. During this time he was well supported by members of the County Council and his family and friends, all of which sustained him. Without such support, these types of events are often very difficult to weather.

This story also has a happy ending in that the County Library Service went on, under Roy's leadership, to become one of the top ones in the country. There is no doubt that this experience, and the strength gained from coping with this calamity stood Roy in good stead for the following many years he spent in his job.

Annotated bibliography and references

Most local authority areas and public organisations will have their own guidelines for best practice in consulting local communities.

Chapter 13

"The importance of pause"

"Life is a series of experiences, each one of which makes us bigger, even though sometimes it is hard to realise this."

Henry Ford

Introduction

The unexpected death of a colleague ranks high on the list of most stressful calamities. And stress is a killer in itself. Despite the predications of an improved work-life balance due to new technology and family-friendly working policies, we find ourselves, nearly twenty years on from this calamity, in working situations which are often no better.

In this chapter, John Guest shares the background to this event and how he reacted to it. An additional complexity for him was the context of public service and the political nature of local government. While many of the political machinations have been excluded from this chapter, you will have no doubt as to the bureaucratic complexities that can be wrought by feuding political parties onto those whose jobs have an urgency.

Key themes

Think before you act

Most disasters are complete surprises. A key leadership skill is the ability to absorb the jolt and then deal with it personally, and with others, in a way that limits any further negative unintended consequences.

Managing stress

John's colleague died of a heart attack at an early age, no doubt brought on, amongst other things, by stress related to his work. Stress is a major killer and contributes to a substantial loss of earnings in business each year. It also diminishes the quality of life of those who experience it at levels beyond what they can cope with either physically or mentally, and also harms their families.

Personal experience

"The disaster was when my friend and colleague the Chief Planner for Greater London died of a heart attack aged 48. His death, apart from of course being extremely sad, created a great difficulty both for Greater London planning and for me personally.

The year was 1986 – a period of political turbulence in London. The Greater London Council was abolished. In an emotive and controversial atmosphere a new group was convened to ensure there was a planning committee for Greater London to produce an urgent plan for London and advise on the most major planning applications.

Appointing a chief planner for Greater London had not been easy. First and foremost this was because a budget could not be agreed due to divided political constituencies within London. It took a significant period to convince the committee that at least agreement should be reached on expenditure for the appointment of a chief planner. When he was finally in post he was a very much-needed man. His death occurred just months after his appointment when he was about to produce his first major reports.

That left me in a very tricky position. On the day of his death he was the only paid officer working for the committee. I was secretary to the committee but this was an honorary post. The only other posts were also honorary i.e. honorary treasurer and honorary legal advisor. It fell to me to deal with the situation. Even before the appointment of the chief planner I had civil servants on my back about the delays and there were threats of the government taking its own action. If they did there was going to be mayhem, for me included. Another problem was I was newly appointed as Chief Executive of a London Borough that was more than a full time job in itself. Having to spend significantly more time on Greater London matters at that point in time would generate serious difficulties.

By bizarre coincidence six more officers to the committee were to take up their posts on the day after the chief planner died. But as a group they had as yet little knowledge of Greater London's current planning problems [compensation arrangements had discouraged many former GLC planners from applying] and the idea was the chief planner was going to mould them into a team, using his knowledge to support them. Without him the new appointees, all very concerned, stood little chance of making early headway, yet the pressures were great.

After taking a degree in law and qualifying as a solicitor John pursued a career in Local Government. He became a District Council Chief Executive in 1974. Twelve years later be became Chief Executive of a London Borough with many additional responsibilities for Greater London matters.

Years earlier I had a conversation with the famous surgeon Sir Ludwig Guttman about spinal injuries and paralysis. He said that very often the accident causing the basic injury did not cause paralysis; tragically it was the actions of those going to the person's aid that did do, for example, by attempting to move an injured patient without knowing how to do so. I never forgot the point he made. I reminded myself that if you have a disaster your reactions to it might have more disastrous consequences than the original disaster. You will often be in a position where you can maximise or minimise the disaster by the actions you take.

From the point of view of dealing with this calamity I was fortunate it happened on a Sunday. That meant that I didn't need to react as quickly as might otherwise have been the case. Looking back that was very important. Immediate action looks impressive but can later be seen by yourself to be hasty ill advised action. But, as we all know, one of the problems with being the person mainly responsible for dealing with or advising on a disaster is that all eyes are on you.

Decisive action is important and the pressure is on you to be seen to take it. Any sign of dithering may cause others to try to intervene and this could lead to serious loss of reputation. Looking back on the calamity of the death of the chief planner I have no doubt that following such a disaster which will be of interest to many, including the press, you need to find some way of spending a couple of hours sitting down and writing out a list of the implications of the disaster before committing yourself to any view. The need to be seen to be decisive must take second place to trying to ensure that the reaction is the correct one. Some implications are not immediately obvious but may have an important influence on what is the right thing to do.

Another important point I note when looking back is that because the disaster impinged on me personally, account had to be taken of the emotional effect on me. The chief planner, Edmund, had been a good friend of mine. I had not known him before his appointment but afterwards we spent much time together, including commuting together. I had driven him home on the Friday two days before his death. He had been white with anger because vital urgent reports he had done had not been printed by the Borough printing section. He was new to the Borough and had not taken the correct steps to book a printing slot. The printing section would not budge because if Edmund's job was done it would then exceed the deadline for another, booked job. By chance I was not in my office at the time. Shamefully I look back on that

The Health & Safety Executive (UK) defines stress as "the adverse reaction people have to excessive pressure or other types of demands placed on them."

Their research indicates that up to 10% of the population (5 million) feel "very" or "extremely" stressed by their work, and that around 500,000 people believe this stress is making them ill.

The total cost to society of work related stress is estimated to be around £3.7 billion (1995/6 prices).

The HSE has published Draft Management Standards to help reduce stress in the workplace:
www.hse.gov.uk/stress/stresspilot/standards.htm

as lucky for me because Edmund would have contacted me as the Borough Chief Executive leaving me with the certain need to refuse to intervene. I am in no doubt that Edmund's anger on that Friday was the immediate cause of his death on the Sunday and I was at least spared the trauma of believing that I had been a direct cause of his death. Nevertheless I knew that he had been working night and day and that this would have some impact on his health. Also due to my role as secretary to the committee I had necessarily placed additional pressures on Edmund and took the view that this would have contributed to the causes of his death. When his wife phoned me on that Sunday morning to say he had died just a few hours earlier I was seriously affected.

We are all human. To be honest both my heart (physically) and my mind were racing, and my judgement, concentration and memory were in danger of being affected. I am convinced that if humanly possible significant decisions and actions should be avoided while you're in such a state. You have consciously to take a strong grip on yourself and be determined to concentrate on the issues in hand before doing so.

I would also observe from my experience that in a disaster full use has to be made of the sympathy factor. People will make allowances and co-operate more than usual following a calamity. It can seem like a cheat to take advantage of a disaster to win a point or a concession but often the circumstances leave you seeking any positive aspect you can get. I found this sympathy factor short-lived and you have to react soon to make the most of it.

Finally, my experience suggests that the list of implications you make should be as comprehensive as possible. Then the list can be structured to distinguish between those requiring immediate action and those that can be left to get more information on or to sleep on. My belief is that Sir Ludwig Guttman's point has a wider connection to how we act following a disaster and the ability we have to make the situation better – or worse.

> "Should you shield the canyons from the windstorms, you would never see the beauty of their carvings."
>
> Elisabeth Kubler-Ross

> Think back to when you had to cope with someone dying or going off ill quite suddenly. What was your immediate reaction? With hindsight, how do you feel this impacted the resolution of the problem?

Think before you act

In times of crisis, the decision-making processes we usually rely on may not be appropriate. On hearing about the calamity our head and heart usually register '*shock*' followed by '*disbelief*' as we try to digest what has happened. As John noted in his reflective sharing, this is not a good time to be in front of the media or making instant decisions you may later regret.

'Guilt' and *'blame'* are the next stages in coping with shock and again, this is an important time for the leader to focus on the issues at hand and not to get stuck in a negative cycle of blaming himself or others for what happened. It is a necessary stage to move through and one that leads to the final stages of *'rationalisation'* and *'integration'*. Here, as we see in John's story, is the ability to see the whole, to bring it together as one story.

In the aftermath of a calamity, decisions are usually required quickly. Finding the time and space to work through what might be most appropriate action is important. This time might be only two hours, but it will be two hours well spent.

A systematic approach to decision making (Smith) is:

1. **Setting objectives**; what do you need to achieve in what timescale? Can you differentiate between short-term urgent decisions that need to be made immediately and those that can be put off until later?
2. **Collecting information**; what information do you need and from whom can you get it at short notice?
3. **Identifying alternative solutions**; before shooting from the hip, what other ways can the problem be handled?
4. **Evaluating options**; which is the best way to go and why?
5. **Selecting the best option**; which one is suitable right now and how will you evaluate its worth? What actions will you have in reserve just in case something goes wrong again?

> Recall the last decision you made very quickly.
>
> Now run through the list above and think through whether you would now do something differently.

Managing stress

Stress is unique to each person and its source is equally varied by what it is that is causing the stress and the ability of the person to cope. Not all stress is bad – we need a certain amount to be able to function. The key to managing your stress is to discover the limits of your personal danger zone, and to recognise when you're there and to take action. Sometimes this action may be drastic, like changing job, or other times it may be no more than taking a day off or signing up with the local education centre to take the evening course you've been meaning to do for ages.

> "The bow too tensely strung is easily broken."
>
> Publius Syrus

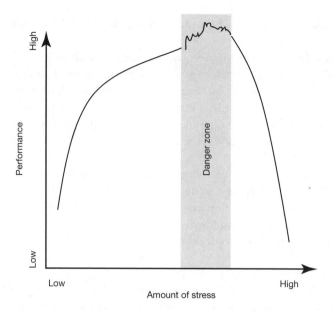

Are you in the danger zone?

Are you experiencing one or more of these factors?

- You are becoming ill more often than before
- You are preoccupied with your own thoughts
- You are seeing less of your friends and family than before
- You are becoming more irritable more often
- You are working longer hours but accomplishing less
- You are tired all the time

Some hints and tips for managing your stress

- Break up your working day; take frequent short breaks so you have time to clear your head
- Learn to manage your time effectively
- Find an exercise regime that works for you
- Reduce the intensity of tasks causing a stress overload – manage them in small chunks over a longer period of time
- Learn to say 'no' and avoid taking on others' responsibilities
- Practise the art of delegation and letting go of anything that doesn't need your constant, personal attention
- If in doubt, have a medical check up

What are your danger zone 'hot buttons?

What stresses you most?

Think through how you might manage this in the future?

Identify at least one thing you have taken on in the last week where you feel you could have said 'no' and thus relieved your pressure a little.

Conclusion

In this very honest and reflective chapter, John has shared the details of a calamity of the most significance – the death of a colleague and friend. With time he has had the opportunity to reflect on what he has learnt about himself and others.

In contrast to Mr X's need to make a decision quickly (see Chapter 8), John's experience was that by slowing down, taking a breath, pausing, he was better able to take stock of the situation and decide what would be the most appropriate course of action. The circumstances and context demanded this decision-making strategy.

Speed is not just an issue for decision-making. Our lives are galloping as we try and keep pace with the technology and demands placed on us by colleagues, friends and family members. Stressors are continually on the increase, not just at the office but also in daily life, and therefore the need to manage stress becomes more and more important. If we don't develop stress management techniques, then we're not going to be very effective. The next generation of leaders may well prove to be those who have found the inner strength and outer serenity to manage their stress positively.

Annotated bibliography and references

30 minutes ... To make the Right Decision by Jane Smith, 1997 is a very short introductory book that won't take you more than half and hour to read.

Effective decision making; A guide to thinking for management success by John Adair, 1985 is a thought provoking if by now slightly elderly approach to decision making!

What stresses us and how we respond to it is very personal. Depending on your tastes, consider the following to help you unwind – a search in any online or high street bookstore will provide you with a number of options:

- Self help book on stress

- Audio CDs or tapes that contain only relaxing music or go for those that also include various types of relaxation and visualisation programmes

Chapter 14

"Rain or shine"

"You should treat all disasters as if they were trivialities but never treat a triviality as if it were a disaster."

Quentin Crisp

Introduction

We end this book with a short and light hearted story from Ian Bond about how he coped, or didn't, in the pouring rain while trying to record the lap times for walkers raising money by walking round a measured track.

Key themes

Be prepared

Baden Powell was right; the more prepared we are, the less surprised we'll be when adversity strikes and the more able we'll be to cope with what it is that has come our way. For the British, carrying an umbrella, even when setting out on a sunny morning, comes from the experience of having been caught out by the fickleness of our weather one time too many.

Finding the funny side in it all

At the time, every calamity, by definition, is an uncomfortable and distressful event, some more so than others. It is on reflection, often in the company of others, that we can look back and see the funny aspects to what happened. Humour is an excellent way of reducing stress and we should not feel ashamed of giving in to it if it feels appropriate.

Personal experience

After Army National Service in 1948, Ian undertook studies at the Royal Dental Hospital, London, and qualified as a dental surgeon in 1955.

There he met his future wife Kathleen, who also qualified at the same time. They married and set up in General Practice in the London Borough of Hillingdon from 1955 through to 1987 when he retired.

During this time he was also a Justice of the Peace (Magistrate) on the Uxbridge Bench.

"After a few minutes the plastic cover was not doing its job, and trying to mark each lap with the pen just tore through wet paper, so keeping the lap chart was impossible. It had turned into one of those nightmare events where charity walkers were attempting to do forty laps round a track in what had, half an hour ago, turned into a major thunderstorm.

This was the third time my wife and I had been asked to help check the laps of each walker as they passed by the finishing line. The first time it was a lovely summer afternoon and people of all ages, including my daughter Sarah, came to walk for charity. Other helpers provided me with cups of tea and cool drinks during the afternoon. By the end of the event I had spent a very pleasant day watching others do the hard work.

As we were leaving we were asked if we would like to help at the next arranged walk. We said yes, not expecting weather that was rather less kind, though manageable. Armed with umbrella and raincoat I managed to get through the afternoon in relative comfort and most of the walkers completed the 10-mile course.

I, of course, agreed to help out at the next event that was the one that turned out to be graced with torrential rain. What amazed me was the spirit of the walkers who were still arriving in great numbers. Two young boys walked together. One asked me how many laps he had done and I said "10". Later on the other boy asked the same question and I said "14".

He replied, "But my friend has done 16."

"That's correct," I said, adding 2 more laps to his total on my soaked sheet.

"Life doesn't require that we do our best – only that we try our best."

H. Jackson Brown Jr.

I found that if I held the lap chart under the table and bent down to look under the table to enter each lap I could keep a reasonable record. It's possible that had I thought about it, I could have come more prepared for the weather and designed a way to record the laps that did not include paper and pen.

Attempts were made by the organisers to give us hot drinks, but as soon as the cup was put down to enter a lap it was blown away. I wished I had brought my own supply in a heavy flask.

At the end of the afternoon, very few walkers had given up and most completed the full 40 laps.

I have not been asked to assist again, but perhaps the organisers are giving me time for the memory to fade."

Recall a time when you were caught out by the weather.

How prepared were you?

Be prepared

The problem with the notion of being prepared is knowing what we are preparing ourselves *for*! If Ian knew there were going to be thunderstorms he might have thought about it for a while and worked out that taking his own flask of coffee would have been a good thing to do. Mind you, he did have some experience of wet weather so he might have had some advance warning.

If we're unprepared then we get surprised and that leads to stress that may mean a reduced ability to cope with the calamity at hand. One way to manage this is to focus on the surprise and reduce these by thinking through the various scenarios that could happen. Thinking through the possibilities might just be enough to trigger a response to take along extra supplies, leave a contact phone number, decide not to go etc.

> Think of an event you are attending in the next month or so.
>
> What could go wrong? Try and come up with at least four or five different scenarios.
>
> How might you minimise your surprises and how can you increase your being prepared to cope?

Finding the funny side of it all

Ian ends his story with a wry remark, gently poking fun at what happened and how he and others coped.

Humour is very specific to its context and the people involved. What is funny for one person may not be appreciated by another. However, the ability to laugh at ourselves, to see the mud on our trousers when we've fallen in a puddle and laugh rather than scream, is one of the saving graces of our human nature. It may mean the difference between coping with the calamity, and not coping.

> Recall an incident you were involved in that made you laugh.
>
> Feel the smile come back. Now close you eyes and remember what the laughter felt like.

Conclusion

All learning is experiential. Even what we learn in books needs to be tested out in the real world. Every day we are afforded opportunities to grow and develop, to learn more and more how to cope with calamities – of whatever magnitude.

Annotated bibliography and references

C.W. Metcalf & R Felible, *Lighten Up: Survival Skills for People Under Pressure* Addison Wesley Longman Publishing Co: A William Patrick Book; 1992

> This book is an easy to read guide to using laughter as a way of becoming more productive, resilient, and stress-free. It demonstrates specific skills and proven techniques to develop and maintain a healthy sense of humour and perspective amidst crises.

About Rotary

ROTARY INTERNATIONAL, established in 1905, is a world wide Service Club, whose members include those men and women who are in leading positions in their chosen careers.

At the end of 2001 there were some 1,188,492 members belonging to 30,149 clubs spread throughout 162 countries. The object of Rotary is:

> To encourage and foster the ideal of service as a basis of worthy enterprise and, in particular to encourage and foster:
> 1. The development of acquaintance as an opportunity for service.
> 2. High ethical standards in business and professions; the recognition of the worthiness of all useful occupations; and the dignifying by each Rotarian of his occupation as an opportunity to serve society.
> 3. The application of the ideal of service by every Rotarian to his personal, business and community life.
> 4. The advancement of international understanding, goodwill, and peace through a world fellowship of business and professional men and women united in the ideal of service.

ROTARY FOUNDATION is Rotary's own CHARITY and operates internationally. Foundation's ambitious programme includes a very wide range of activities comprising:

> Polio Plus, Health, Hunger and Humanity (3-H) Grants, Matching Grants, Helping Grants, New Opportunities Grants, Rotary Peace Programmes, Grants for Rotary Volunteers, Discovery Grants, Disaster Relief Grants, Community Assistance Programme Grants, Humanitarian Transportation Grants, Ambassadorial Scholarships, Rotary Grants for University Teachers, and Group Study Exchange.

Of these, Polio Plus is both the largest and most ambitious of Rotary's programmes. The aim is the eradication of Polio throughout the world by 2005 to celebrate Rotary's own centenary. By that time it is anticipated that through the efforts of Rotary, Foundation will have contributed in excess of half a billion US$ providing oral polio vaccine to over two billion children by the giving of grants to 122 nations around the world.

The author's royalties from this book will all be donated to Rotary Foundation through the Rotary Club of Aylesbury.

THE ROTARY CLUB OF AYLESBURY is the local club of which the author is a member. The Club is one of the oldest clubs in the UK having been founded in 1924. There are some 40 members from whom these experiences all come and which includes a very active local Foundation Committee.

In addition to the Foundation Committee there are a number of other committees:

- Club Service, which is responsible for the good operation of the Club
- Community Service, which is responsible for local projects
- International Service, which is responsible for overseas projects
- Vocational Service, which is responsible for youth activities
- Charity Funds, which raises money for each of the above committees

Membership of Rotary is not about giving money, it is about giving service. The value comes from peoples' experiences and their contacts thus making things happen. These aims are the aims of all Rotary clubs around the world.

At the end of 2003 Rotary International had 1,227,545 members in 31,561 clubs in 166 countries.